Lamotrek Atoll and Inter-Island Socioeconomic Ties

LAMOTREK ATOLL
AND INTER-ISLAND
SOCIOECONOMIC TIES

William H. Alkire
University of Victoria

WAVELAND
PRESS, INC.
Prospect Heights, Illinois

For information about this book, write or call:

Waveland Press, Inc.
P.O. Box 400
Prospect Heights, Illinois 60070
(847) 634-0081

Cover Two canoes anchored off Pugue where laborers from Lamotrek have travelled to make copra. Chief Igefail in the foreground.

Frontispiece At the end of a communal labor project an exchange of gifts occurs between the men and women of Lamotrek. Men present bottles of sweet coconut toddy to the women and receive cooked taro and breadfruit in return.

7 6

Foreword

William Alkire spent 15 months living with the 200 persons who inhabit the small atoll of Lamotrek, which is one of the Western Caroline Islands of Micronesia. The present monograph analyzes the patterns of subsistence activities and social and religious life of these people, but it also provides new insights into special facets of the cultural ecological adaptations which perpetuate close ties between all of these islands. Underlying the inter-island social and political relations is a mutual dependency necessitated by the frequent disasters in this area of tropical storms and typhoons.

Lamotrek is one of some 15 low-lying atolls which are fairly closely spaced. It is so inseparably bound to Elato and Satawal, which are respectively 15 and 40 miles away, that Alkire considers that these three islands constitute a "single social system." All of these atolls or "outer islands," however, have been described by some authors as parts of the "Yapese Empire," although Yap is nearly 600 miles to the west. This rather euphemistic statement of the role of Yap is based on the continued political, social, religious, and economic superiority which the outer islands accord Yap.

The inter-island dependencies follow traditional patterns of duties and obligations which are determined by the widely spread system of ranked clans, political dominance within lineages of high status, strong ritualism and priesthoods, and economic exchange. Where inter-island voyages are comparatively easy, as in the case of Lamotrek, Satawal, and Elato, exchange of goods through reciprocal obligations and exchange of people through marriage patterns is continuous. This situation is not unlike that of continual societies whose members inter-relate with one another through various patterns even though the total society occupies a large territory. The continued ties of these atolls with islands farther away, especially with Yap, is, however, more difficult to understand. It would seem that the historically derived or traditional patterns would become attenuated with distance to the point that inter-island obligations would fade into nothing.

Alkire has returned to the Western Carolines to analyze further the problem of how extensive and intimate inter-island ties may be in terms of the distances separating islands or clusters of islands. Meanwhile, his present findings, although somewhat provisional, demonstrate clearly that sheer physical survival would be virtually impossible if each atoll were entirely independent of others and could not seek help in extreme emergencies.

Two very different types of islands are involved in the survival problems of the Carolines. None of the atolls in the storm belt comprises more than a few square miles, has a population of over 200 or 300, or rises more than a few feet above sea level. High seas may sweep entirely across them, laying waste their land resources and killing their people. Yap, by contrast, is a high volcanic island of about 80 square miles and has a population of nearly 5,000 people. It is less damaged by seas, its people may find refuge from storms, and it recovers in time from high winds.

The clustered atolls in the eastern portion of the Western Carolines can maintain fairly close and permanent ties with one another owing to the fairly short sea voyages. If several adjacent atolls are simultaneously stricken, their inhabitants may go farther afield for help. The need for interdependency is so great that if the present patterned system of mutual obligations did not exist some comparable system would certainly have been developed. That the insurance provisions of the inter-island relationships operate within historically derived institutions makes them no less effective. It is, in fact, tempting to speculate that the very pattern of ranked clans, subclans, and lineages may be an expression of economic dependency. The more secure islands assist the stricken atolls not only by furnishing goods but by supplying people who help restore the decimated populations. The relationship thus would tend somewhat to polarize differences between the givers and receivers, wherein the clans of the former might well acquire superordinate statuses.

These hints concerning the possible origins of the status system are of course purely speculative, for a generally similar social structure is widely spread throughout the Pacific. Its genesis lies far back in history, perhaps in areas where the factor of insurance against disaster had little importance. At the same time, it is significant that Yap is the last resort. Despite its distance from most of the atolls, assistance from Yap in time of need was assured by one or more voyages each year which were made partly to affirm its dominant position.

The nature of atoll society and inter-island relations described by Alkire appears to be essentially aboriginal or pre-contact in the area. Yap has been subjected to control by various foreign nations and to strong influences from outside trade. The outer islands are too small and too remote to have attracted many outside visitors. The copra trade has touched Lamotrek only lightly, and metal tools have been acquired only to a limited extent. As Alkire's text and photographs indicate, subsistence patterns and the general way of life are still aboriginal.

The principal effect of outside contact has been the introduction of diseases which, together with natural disasters, has brought great population decline. Lamotrek's population was estimated to have been about 2,000 in 1800. Although this figure is, as Alkire indicates, suspect—it would give a density of 8,000 people per square mile, since Lamotrek has only one-quarter square mile of land—the atoll had 300 people in 1890 and has little more than 200 today. Satawal had 900 persons in 1800, 200 in 1890, and 300 today. Elato has only 50 people today. Deaths, whether through disease, storms, or loss of canoe loads of men at sea, may virtually wipe out certain clans and subclans, leaving a social imbalance that affects the entire system of reciprocity. The balance may, however, be restored through intermarriages or movements of large groups of people to depopulated atolls. A flexible system of land use and tenure facilitates these readjustments.

Alkire's analysis does not presuppose that insurance against disaster was an important factor in social relationships elsewhere. It does suggest, however, that small and vulnerable populations may have been linked to one another and to larger, more stable societies in other parts of the Pacific for similar reasons. Whether such interdependencies exist on any large scale in continental societies remains in doubt. In certain organized states, such as the Inca Empire, food was stored and distributed in case of need by the central government. Among societies that were based essentially upon kinship ties, we know that food was shared with close relatives and sometimes fellow villagers. It is interesting that most forms of cooperation between closely related societies or segments of any one society pertain to production far more than consumption. Interfamilial labor exchange in farming rarely extends to division of the harvest. Cooperative hunting, as in the case of bison hunts, is a matter of organized killing, wherein division of the game follows only as part of the food-getting operation. Perhaps there is something about people and their cultures that has accorded more importance to the producer, whether he be hunter, farmer, or manufacturer, than to the consumer. Today we think of the taxpayer as separable from the beneficiary and of intricately organized institutions as appropriate to producers rather than to consumers. In view of what are essentially consumers' insurance cooperatives in the Western Caroline Islands, one wonders whether this aspect of human relationships may not have been somewhat overlooked elsewhere.

Alkire's analysis has, I think, an even wider implication for ethnographic studies. Not so many years ago, the ideal ethnography tended to view a society as a closed system. Although it was obvious that such matters as warfare involved external relationships, the full meaning of such relationships was rarely examined. The tendency today is to understand any social system as a response to its adjustments to its natural environment and to its external social environment. Each study discloses new ways in which the larger context of a society may affect its fundamental nature.

JULIAN H. STEWARD

Acknowledgments

This investigation was supported by a fellowship (M-12,068) and a research grant (M-5125) from the National Institute of Mental Health, Public Health Service.

This monograph was originally submitted to the Graduate College of the University of Illinois in partial fulfillment of the requirements for a Ph.D. degree in anthropology. I would like to thank the members of my thesis committee—J. B. Casagrande, D. B. Shimkin, E. M. Bruner, F. K. Lehman, A. W. Booth—and especially my chairman, J. H. Steward.

The administrative personnel of the Trust Territory of the Pacific Islands arranged transportation while in the field and offered their facilities for gathering background material. Special thanks are given to Mr. Harry Uyehara (Director of Education, Yap District), Bernard You and Antonio Golbau (Yap District Hospital), Mr. William Monahan (U.S. Weather Bureau, Guam), and LCDR John Kearney (U.S.S. *Haverfield*).

Mr. E. H. Bryan, Jr., Manager of the Pacific Scientific Information Center, Bishop Museum, offered his help in locating maps of the Western Caroline area. The base maps included herein are drawn from field maps made by the author and from U.S. Hydrographic Office nautical charts 6042, 5425, and 5417.

My greatest thanks, however, are given to the people of Lamotrek, Elato, and Satawal, to whom I dedicate this volume—*hasa hashigüshig reimelap.*

Contents

1

Introduction

THE PROBLEM

The inhabitants of the many small atolls and islands of the Western Pacific rarely constitute wholly independent economic, social, and political societies despite their comparative isolation from one another over many miles of ocean. Island populations in anthropological research are often studied, however, from the viewpoint that the society is synonymous with the island, but few islands of the world—even aboriginally—have been completely isolated. This work, which is an analysis of structure and not of content, is primarily concerned with the people of Lamotrek Atoll in the Western Caroline Islands of Micronesia. In this case, though, the society in question is not limited to this island alone, but comprises that population which interacts in terms of a single pattern and thus embraces several other islands of the area as well. If the study of the social organization of this area were not defined in this broader sense and groups of islands were not treated as participating in cohesive social systems, then inter-island communication and exchange—although often reported for the area—would remain unexplained. A fundamental premise of this study is that inter-island modes of interaction are of the same social structure as that which organizes activities of the residents of a single island within an interacting group. Uberoi (1962) has demonstrated the value of this approach in his recent reanalysis of the political aspects of the *kula*

1

(Malinowski 1961), and Davenport (1964) has noted the presence of similar systems elsewhere in Melanesia.

The following factors will emerge in the course of this analysis:

1. *There are features of the natural environmental setting of the Western Carolines which encourage the development of a system of inter-island social ties.* Among such environmental characteristics are (a) the restricted land areas of the Western Caroline Islands, (b) the limited range of agricultural staples available, (c) the hazards and uncertainties of marine exploitation, and, most important, (d) the destructive effects of tropical storms.

Human survival on the coral islands of the Western Carolines is precarious owing to the low elevation of the land area above sea level and the frequent ravages of tropical storms. When natural disaster diminishes the food supply and threatens the survival of a population, the people often take refuge upon or seek assistance from neighboring islands and atolls with which they maintain ties of reciprocity. Lamotrek, like most other small islands of the area, is reasonably fertile under normal conditions and its resources have often supported a fairly dense population and relatively complex local kinship, political, and religious systems. But destruction of resources has been sufficiently frequent for survival to have required that Lamotrek and other islands be linked by systems of mutual economic aid, which, in turn, have involved kinship and other ties. The establishment of inter-island bonds allows a wider distribution of economic goods and hence a greater resource base than that available to any single island. In this way, any shortage, whether due to the individual characteristics of a particular island or to the effects of a natural disaster, can be offset by dependence upon materials obtained from another island within the network. If such exchange is to occur smoothly a structured means of dealing with the situation is necessary. The superior position of Yap among the Western Caroline Islands (which is described more fully below) is not the result of mere conquest—although this island may have used such force at times in the past—but rather of the greater abundance and reliability of its resources, which have given it a prominence in a reciprocal system.

2. *One of the main characteristics of the social organization of these islands is flexibility in adapting to changing conditions by recognizing legitimate alternatives of action.* This fact is directly related to the need of Western Carolinian social organization to be

adapted to an environment which might unexpectedly and rapidly change. When, later in the text, the problems of depopulation, land tenure and inheritance, inter-island exchange of economic goods and personnel, and the integration of foreign influences are discussed, alternative choices sanctioned by the traditional social organization should be evident. The particular course of action followed depends on the existing complex of circumstances. For example, the fact that normally "Course A" would prevail 80 per cent of the time does not mean that "Course B," chosen the other 20 per cent of the time—when altered conditions exist—is any less traditional or legitimate. A structural analysis can only be considered complete when it encompasses all legitimate cultural alternatives related to the complex of circumstances in which they occur.

3. *Contact with world powers has, thus far, resulted in few fundamental structural changes in Western Carolinian atoll society.* If one were to assume that the traditional culture under consideration were that of a single island's people, then certain features of contemporary social organization on Lamotrek, for example, might be explained as changes brought about by contact with foreign powers. Thus, they could be classified as symptomatic of a breakdown in traditional cultural organization. However, when the islands of the Western Carolines are viewed as components of a larger social system, where socioeconomic decisions are often made on an inter-island level, many of the trends in recent cultural change are no more than adjustments to and integration of new environmental conditions through means contained within the traditional structure.

Foreign administrative influence has, for all practical purposes, replaced Yapese suzerainty over the outer islands. Contact between the outer islands and the administering government has never been frequent. The resources available in the outer islands for exploitation were not of such value or quantity as to warrant forced cultural changes by an administration. Thus, there has been no alteration in the islanders' basic reliance on a subsistence economy. The appearance of foreign administrators can be viewed as merely another environmental change—a substitution of Japanese or Americans for Yapese. Even the depopulation which occurred, directly and indirectly, because of this contact was not an event completely alien to the Western Carolinians. Conditions which often led to food and resource shortages also reduced or limited the population numbers of an island. Hence, post-contact depopulation did not result in a breakdown of traditional social organization; the means for the orderly integration of such change were contained in the existing social system.

In summary, this analysis will show that the societies of Lamotrek, Elato, and Satawal are components in a single social system. Many of the features of the local social organization of each can only be adequately explained with reference to this larger supra-island structure, and, furthermore, the processes involved in cultural change, whether stimulated internally or externally, can only be understood as taking place in the context of an inter-island organization.

THE WESTERN CAROLINE ISLANDS

For the purposes of this work I shall hereafter refer to all islands from Yap to Namonuito as the Western Caroline Islands.

Aboriginally, a network of outlying low coral islands and atolls was presided over by Gagil District on the volcanic island of Yap. The islands of Ulithi, Fais, Sorol, Woleai, Eauripik, Ifaluk, Faraulep, Elato, Lamotrek, Satawal, Puluwat, Pulusuk, Pulap, and Namonuito (Map 1) were linked to Yap by a system of political, economic, and religious ties.

Lessa (1950), from information gathered on Ulithi, reconstructed the system in some detail as it existed in the recent past. His article, which is primarily concerned with Ulithian-Yapese relationships, deals with the political center of the network. Lessa's analysis should be consulted for many details, for I shall only restate here those aspects of the system which directly relate to the islands at the eastern periphery of Yapese control.

Subservience to Yap was evidenced in the following way. All of the outer islands, at specified intervals, were obliged to send objects of tribute (*pitigil tamol*) to the chief of Gagil District on Yap. In addition, outer island representatives presented religious gifts (*mepel*) to the head religious functionary of Gagil, and *sawei* gift exchange occurred between the peoples of the outer islands and specific Yapese "overlords."

Originating on individual outer islands, the aforementioned material flowed in a specified way from islands of low status through those of equal or higher standing until it reached the Yapese of

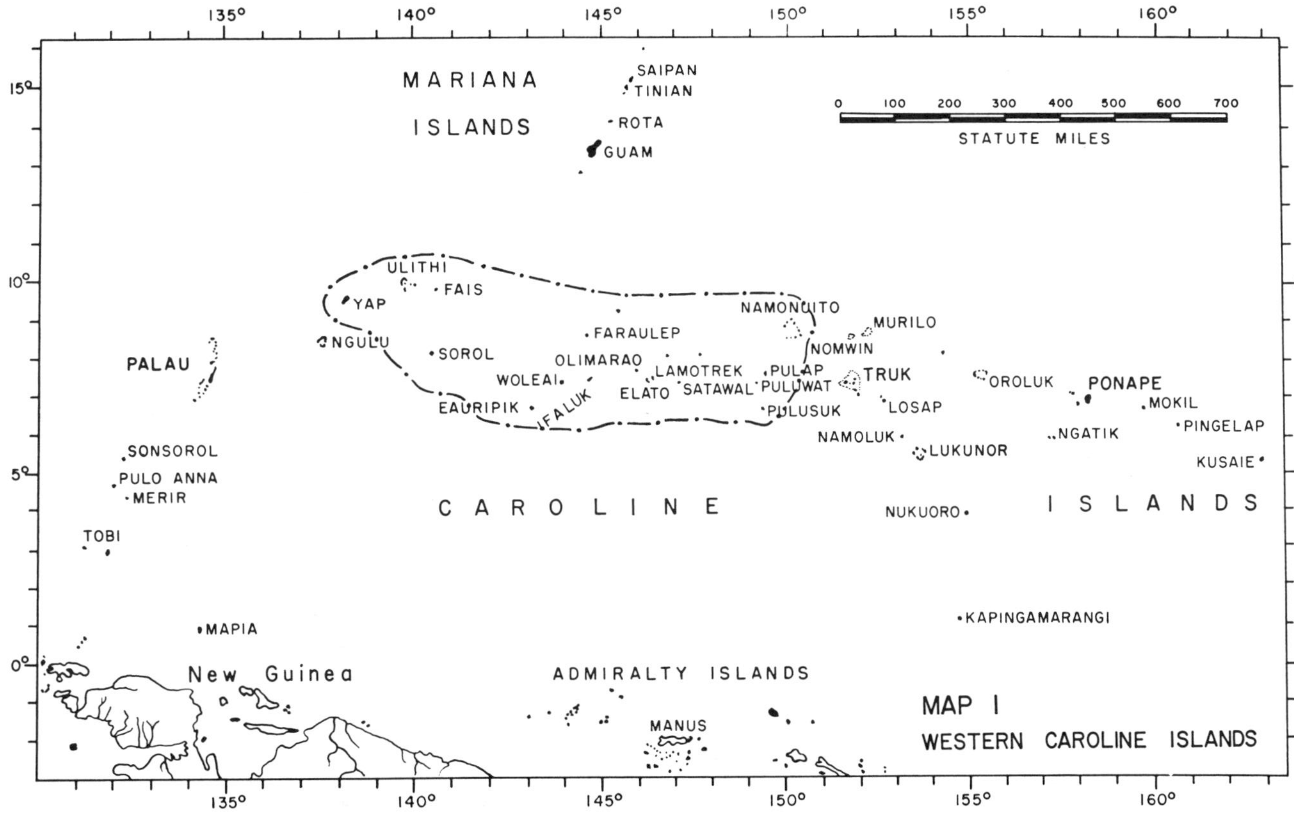

MAP I
WESTERN CAROLINE ISLANDS

Gatchepar Village, Gagil District. A representative of each island atoll would usually accompany the tribute of his island. At each intermediate island, the chief with the highest rank was in charge of the whole expedition. For this reason the chief of Mogmog, Ulithi, who represented the highest-ranking outer island, made the tribute presentation to the Yapese chief when the canoe fleet landed. This superior status of Mogmog among the outer islands also meant that any political or religious directives Yap wished to send to any outer island were always relayed through this Ulithian chief.

Puluwat, Pulusuk, Pulap, and Namonuito, all islands at the eastern periphery of Yapese control, ceased to participate in tribute payments sometime during German administration of the Carolines (1899-1914). Lessa (1950) states that among the remaining outer islands, though, the system began to atrophy only during Japanese (1914-45) and American (1945 to present) periods of administration. He cites four reasons for the declining influence of Yap over her former "Empire": (1) a Japanese prohibition on distant inter-island canoe travel disrupted communication; (2) the advent of Christianity removed traditional Yapese sanctions; (3) introduction of general education by foreign administrations reoriented islanders' thinking; (4) depopulation on Yap resulted in a scarcity of individuals able to fulfill the reciprocal obligations of *sawei* (Lessa 1950: 50).

One might assume that with this decline of influence and power at the political center, the total system of inter-island ties would disintegrate. Such an assumption would only be justified if the network were considered wholly of a hierarchical political and religious nature, held together by the leadership of Yap. The evidence to be presented herein should demonstrate that the basis of the system was not Yapese domination. Thus, even though Yapese control has largely disappeared, the basic ties between outer islands persist.

Any attempt to determine how Yap came to extend its political domination over the outer islands would not be profitable so long after the origin of the system and, especially now, after its decline. On the other hand, because basic inter-island ties persist, at least among outer islanders, it is reasonable to assume that the conditions which have promoted their persistence from the start may not have changed. An attempt will be made to delineate the basis of these inter-island ties and their relationship both to Western

Carolinian social organization as a whole and to the environment in which they function.

RESEARCH PROCEDURES

The islands here chosen for intensive analysis have been purposely selected from among those at the periphery of former Yapese influence. A view from this outlying region may more readily expose certain basic structural features which might otherwise be obscured by superficial elements in islands closer to the center of political influence.

Lamotrek was chosen as the main island for field work not only because of its distance from Yap and Ulithi, but also because it is the politically superior island of the peripheral group which now includes Elato and Satawal and which once included islands farther east.

Fifteen months, from March, 1962, to June, 1963, were spent on Lamotrek, including side trips of three weeks to Elato, two and a half weeks to Satawal, and one week to Olimarao. Comparative data were also gathered on Lamotrek from Elatoan and Satawalese visitors.

Prior to arriving on Lamotrek a month had been spent consulting Yap Trust Territory Administration files on the outer islands. Several Yapese in Gatchepar and Wanyan villages of Gagil District were also interviewed at that time.

On arrival at Lamotrek, in March, 1962, I first conferred with the three district chiefs of the island. At that time I could neither speak nor understand the local language so the meeting was carried out with the aid of an interpreter-assistant I had hired on Ulithi. I had been told by administration officials on Yap that it was highly doubtful that anyone on Lamotrek knew enough English to fill this position. It was decided at this meeting that I should take up residence in the island dispensary (Map 9), a two-room thatched building used for medical storage and by the administration doctors on their periodic visits to the island.

The initial three months of field work were devoted to gathering and recording basic data upon which later intensive work would depend. Lamotrek Island was mapped, using plane table and alidade, and all structures as well as the area of taro cultivation were plotted. I took a census of the island on the basis of which I inserted the boundaries of all residence, or homestead, plots. The boundaries of other land holdings on the island were discovered and noted as time permitted throughout the rest of my stay. It was during these initial months of residence on the island that an intensive effort was made to gain a basic knowledge of the Lamotrekan language.

Records were begun on diet, hours spent in marine and agricultural tasks, travel, and community labor. Although these schedules of information were not religiously kept for my entire stay on the island, mainly because of the pressure of other work, the records for each do span four or more months' time, so that the figures can be projected with some accuracy into yearly averages. Rainfall statistics were kept for the entire 15 months of my residency using a rain gauge lent to me by the U.S. Weather Bureau representative on Yap.

My own participation in local events increased as time went on and my linguistic ability improved. In addition to accompanying the men on a fishing expedition once a week, I made several longer canoe voyages to the uninhabited islands in Elato and Olimarao atolls, either on copra-making or turtle-hunting expeditions. Voyages were also made to Elato and Satawal for the specific purpose of carrying out my own work.

Direct questioning of informants, with and without the aid of an interpreter, provided the detailed information on economic, political, and religious organization. Informants were rewarded with gifts, and, at one time or another during my stay, every individual on the island received a gift. My interpreter-assistant was the only individual to whom I paid a wage, and he was not a local resident.

I soon found that the use of an interpreter from an island other than the one I was working on had distinct disadvantages. First, the dialectal difference between Ulithian and Lamotrekese was great enough to make it difficult and confusing to attempt to learn Lamotrekese with the aid of a Ulithian speaker. It was much easier, and more accurate, to work directly with Lamotrekans, no matter how limited their knowledge of English, than to learn proper Lamotrekese after it had been filtered through a Ulithian. Second, and more important, I found that because of the traditional status distinctions between islands of the Western Carolines, Lamotrekans were often reluctant to speak, frankly or at length, about political or religious concerns in the presence of a Ulithian. When informants were questioned about such matters, and my assistant was present, they would either attempt to learn his feelings on the topic and then voice agreement or, if this were not possible, give a neutral answer which would neither offend a Ulithian nor oppose traditional Ulithian attitudes on the topic.

For these reasons, midway through my field work, I sent this assistant back to his home island. After his departure I found that not only did my linguistic ability accelerate, but also that I was able to gather data on political and religious affairs which had been unobtainable before. I was able to compare Lamotrekan attitudes toward Ulithians which had been expressed when a Ulithian was present on the island with attitudes expressed after this individual had left the island. This proved to be an ideal occasion for comparing observations of political and religious beliefs as professed to a higher-status authority (the Ulithian) with those actually practiced. The experience confirmed some hypotheses and suggested others relevant to Western Carolinian inter-island ties.

2

The Setting

Lamotrek Atoll lies at 7° 30′ N., 146° 20′ E. Elato is 14 nautical miles to the west and Satawal is approximately 40 nautical miles east of Lamotrek. Linguistic and cultural evidence indicates that the settling of these islands occurred from the region of Truk, but a date for this settlement has yet to be determined.

The first recorded European sighting of these islands was made by the English captain, James Wilson, in October of 1797 (Wilson *et al.* 1799:293). There is evidence, however, that the islanders had earlier contact with Europeans, either at Lamotrek itself, or possibly on Guam, to which they often made canoe voyages for the purpose of trade (Lessa 1962b:331).

Krämer (1937:9) mentions several vessels which visited the island subsequent to 1797, but it was not until 1880, when the islands were nominally under Spanish control, that an English trader named Lewis settled on the island and the people of Lamotrek came into prolonged contact with Westerners. Even after Spain sold her Micronesian possessions to Germany in 1899 Krämer states that contact was infrequent up to the time of his arrival in 1909. Krämer was the first ethnologist to visit Lamotrek. He and his wife were on the island from November 21 to December 10, 1909. The results of their work were published in 1937 in a volume of the *Ergebnisse der Südsee Expedition 1908-1910,* edited by G. Thilenius.

In 1914 Germany lost control of the Carolines to Japan as a re-

Plate 1. Lagoon side of Lamotrek Island.

sult of World War I. Subsequently, several Japanese established residence on Lamotrek and Satawal. United States administration of the Carolines, as a part of the United Nations Trust Territory of the Pacific Islands, began in 1945 and continues to the present. Initial administration was by the Navy (Richard 1957) but was later transferred to the Department of the Interior. Since 1945 no American or non-Carolinian had remained on Lamotrek for longer than two or three weeks until this writer arrived there in 1962. One other anthropologist—Shigeru Kaneshiro, an employee of the Trust Territory Government—spent ten days on the island in 1950. At the time of my study an administration copra-trading ship visited the island once every three or four months. The effects of these contacts and of the foreign administration of the area will be discussed in Chapter 7.

One premise of this analysis is that the natural environment of the Western Carolines is not only limited in its range of subsistence resources, but also is subject to rapid or unpredictable change which can threaten the productivity of individual islands or island groups. This chapter will describe that environment in detail.

THE ISLANDS

Island Types

There are three physiographically distinct island types in the Western Carolines. They can be classified as volcanic-continental, coral atoll, and raised coral. The first is often referred to as a "high" island and the latter two collectively called "low" islands. Of those islands which once were included in the Yapese political network Yap itself is the sole example of the volcanic-continental type. Fais and Satawal are raised coral formations. All others are coral atolls.

Subsistence resources on high volcanic islands are usually more numerous and less susceptible to damage as a result of natural disaster than the resources of low islands. In nearly every case the high island has an advantage in size, soil fertility, abundance of fresh water, and protective topographical features which the low islands lack (Barrau 1961:22-33, 67-70). This generalization holds true in all comparisons between Yap and the outlying coral islands of the Western Carolines.

Wiens (1962a) has recently presented a comprehensive summary of coral island environments. Tracey, Abbott, and Arnow (1961) have similarly discussed the geological and geographical characteristics of Ifaluk Atoll. In general, the physiographic features of Lamotrek, Elato, and Satawal are universally associated with islands of their respective types. Nonetheless, every coral island of the Western Carolines has certain unique characteristics which contribute to its habitability and potential productivity. Size, soil type, and topography are of prime importance to these islands.

Land Area

The land area of an atoll is usually directly related to its reef area. Wiens (1962a:41) found, in his survey of Pacific atolls, that

72 per cent had less than half their reef area occupied by land, and of this percentage by far the majority had less than one-third of their rim areas above sea level. In addition, the total land area of an atoll is nearly always divided among several islets, many of which are often too small to invite permanent human occupation.

The largest islets of Carolinian atolls are usually found at the windward end of the reef or at points of sharp curvature of the reef (Wiens 1962a:41, 44). It is in these two areas that storms and currents are most likely to deposit island-building debris.

Ground Water

The availability of fresh water on a coral island is dependent on the island's size (Wiens 1962a: 44, 317-31; Tracey *et al.* 1961:34-44). Ground water on a low island is found in a fresh-water lens (Ghyben-Herzberg lens) that is formed of rain water which, having permeated the soil of the island, floats on top of the heavier salt water beneath the soil surface. The size of this lens of fresh water depends on a number of factors and its edges correspond roughly with the edges of the island. Its depth below the surface is a function of island size and the 40:41 weight differential of fresh and salt water. For every foot above sea level that the fresh-water table is found at the center of the island, the lens will extend 40 feet below sea level (Tracey *et al.* 1961:34). From this point the lens will decrease gradually to nothing at the edges of the island. On Ifaluk it was found that the fresh-water lens was absent where island width dropped to 350 feet; however, it was well developed at a width of 700 feet (Tracey *et al.* 1961:35).

Obviously on an island that is too small to support an adequate ground-water lens, vegetation will either be sparse or nonexistent, and the usefulness of a particular island as a habitat for man will correspondingly be restricted.

Soil Type

Soil types are of no less importance than the presence of ground water for the support of plant life. The most common constituents of atoll island soils are calcium carbonate and magnesium carbonate (Wiens 1962a:334-35). On larger islets an overlay of humus, variable in both depth and location, is usually found. The basic calcium and magnesium carbonate soils are derived from the reef constituents while the humus is the result of decaying organic matter.

Stone (1953:2) noted that "as a source of plant nutrients . . . the calcereous medium tends to be favorable for some nitrogen-fixing legumes and Azotobacter. However, it limits availability of certain nutrients such as iron, of which there is a conspicuous deficiency whenever organic matter content in the soil is low." For this reason, agricultural crops on coral islands can be profitably cultivated only when the organic content of the soil is of sufficient level to inhibit chlorosis, a common plant disease which can be traced either to the high lime content of the soil or to the low iron content (Barrau 1961:68; Wiens 1962a:335). This disease, in its most serious forms, can lead to plant death and often is only avoided by artificial mulching in areas where natural humus content is low.

Topography

Low islands have been so designated after their most outstanding physiographic and topographic characteristic. The highest point of a coral island is rarely greater than 25 feet above sea level, and the average elevation, therefore, is usually much less.

Most of the Pacific coral reefs are probably of Tertiary age (Wiens 1962a:97). The significantly lower sea level of Pleistocene times undoubtedly exposed many of these reefs, and it is at this time that erosional forces began which built up the deposits that now constitute the reef islets. The continuing effects of erosion by sea and wind have added to these deposits, and their main areas of location depend on the patterns of wind, current, and storms. In nearly every case there are certain uniform physiographic and topographic features of coral islands which reflect the pattern of island-building forces. Proceeding from the lagoon side to the ocean side of an atoll island one will usually see a low sandy beach facing on the lagoon which rises to an elevation of approximately six or eight feet. Moving inland, the beach levels off into a plain which either continues beyond the midpoint of the island or decreases in elevation, thus forming a swampy area one or two feet above sea level. Beyond the swamp the land usually rises again at a more rapid rate, reaching its greatest elevation in the vicinity of the ocean beach. The lagoon beach is sandy, the interior swamp chiefly humus, and the ocean side composed primarily of coral cobbles, beach rock, and boulders.

The characteristics of the raised coral island, i.e., an island formed on a submerged and then uplifted reef, is quite similar. The sandy

Plate 2. Ocean side of Lamotrek Island where beach-rock development can be noted.

beach is on the leeward side of the island, since such an island lacks a lagoon, and the interior swampy area may or may not be present depending on the maximum and average elevation of the island.

THE CLIMATE

The weather which is usually encountered on individual islands of this region of the Carolines naturally reflects climatic conditions common to marine-tropical environments. Perhaps the only significant deviation from this rule is in the case of high volcanic islands, which, because of their variation in elevation, may produce localized weather conditions not found over the open ocean of surrounding areas. Low coral islands, whose highest trees rarely reach more than 100 feet above sea level, do not alter air current and cloud conditions enough to result in higher rainfall over their land masses.

Temperature

The average maximum daily temperature ranges between 84° and 88° F. Noon monthly variation is rarely more than three or four degrees. The highest midday temperature recorded on Lamotrek was 93° in May and the lowest was 75° in that same month. Diurnal air temperatures have a greater range than seasonal noon variation; nighttime temperatures may drop six to ten degrees. Water temperatures average in the low and mid 80's for both the lagoon and the ocean (Tracey *et al.* 1961:12). The relative humidity is also high, averaging 80 to 90 per cent in the morning.

Rainfall

Patterns of rainfall show great variation. The rainfall statistics recorded by this writer for the year running from April, 1962, through March, 1963, show a higher total and a greater monthly variation for Lamotrek than those cited by either Krämer (1937:3), 108 inches, or the pre-1943 four-year average of the U.S. Hydrographic Office, 104 inches (Tracey *et al.* 1961:12). The 1962-63 total was 137.07 inches. A high of 16.67 inches fell in December and a low of 4.82 inches in October. This low is still more than twice as high as the February low mentioned by Krämer.

The average monthly rainfall for the year was 11.42 inches. When a seasonal distinction is made, May through October had a 12.66-inch average per month while November through April saw a mean of 10.19 inches. Thus there seems to be no great seasonal variation. The average number of consecutive days, in any one month, with no rain was 3.5 and the longest dry spell of the year occurred in October, when ten days passed with no recorded rain.

Since there was some overlap in the statistics recorded for 1962-63, a significant yearly variation was noted. April, 1962, had 6.90 inches of rain while April of the following year had 12.30 inches; May, 1962, had a total of 15.50 inches while May of 1963 totaled a mere 7.33 inches.

Obviously, rainfall is high, showers are heavy, and long dry spells are infrequent, but seasonal variation is unpredictable. Rainfall is high enough to support and maintain a sufficient ground-water lens on all relatively large coral islands of this region, and, thereby, maintain heavy vegetation which would not otherwise survive in the relatively infertile soils present. Nevertheless, because of the unpredictable dry spells and a rapid percolation rate, low or poorly spaced rainfall can adversely affect crop production in times of crisis. A period of low rainfall on Lamotrek in early 1960, for example, slowed the recovery of coconut trees after the 1958 typhoon (Trust Territory 1960:4).

Wind Patterns

The two seasons of the year which the islands' inhabitants themselves recognize are not wet and dry periods, but seasons of variation in wind direction. The season of east and northeast trade winds runs approximately from November through April, while May through October is characterized by west, southwest, and variable east winds. It is during this latter season that prolonged calms may occur, sometimes ten or more days in length. Even during the trade wind season, unexpected calms may develop. Such calms can be disruptive to fishing expeditions and long-distance canoe travel, as overly strong winds are hazardous. During the 1962-63 year noted above, prolonged calms occurred in October, 1962, and May, 1963; both lasted for more than ten days.

On occasion, during the season of variable winds, a strong and continuous west wind will blow across the lagoon and directly into the village area. Although this has the advantage of keeping flies and mosquitoes down, it has the greater disadvantage of destroying certain agricultural crops, notably papaya trees. These trees may be blown over, since their roots are very shallow, or, more frequently if the wind continues for several days, the salt spray carried by it will kill them. It is for this reason that most coral islands have few such sensitive agricultural crops growing near the windward side of the island.

Typhoons

The wind in its most extreme form, the typhoon, is the most destructive climatic phenomenon of the Western Carolines. Tropical storms and typhoons are an ever present threat in these latitudes and are greatly feared by residents of coral islands.

Although two-thirds of the tropical storms in any one year usually occur from July through October, destructive storms can strike an island in any month. Typhoons, which are tropical storms with winds of 64 knots and above, have occurred 17 or 18 times on the average per year, from 1953 through 1957, in that area of the North Pacific Ocean stretching from the Marshall Islands westward (Wiens 1962a:173). Wiens notes, "sometimes long periods elapse without storms, while at other periods there may be one a year for several years." In general, any storm with winds in excess of 45 knots will cause damage to island vegetation and/or structures.

Even though the time of year in which typhoons occur is unpredictable there does seem to be some consistency in the paths these storms follow. The most frequent area of origin for tropical storms in the North Pacific is between five and ten degrees north latitude (Wiens 1962a:174). In the Western Pacific storms travel westerly and northwesterly, most often reaching typhoon proportions somewhere between 140° and 150° E. There are two main paths which they then follow in the Western Carolines. One is taken by those storms which have their origin in the vicinity of Truk; they generally travel in a northwesterly direction, passing in the vicinity of Guam. The other path is followed by those storms which originate south of Truk around Lukunor and travel on a more west-by-north path toward Yap and Ulithi. This latter course often carries such storms directly over Satawal, Lamotrek, and Elato (Map 2).

In the years from 1953 through 1957 four tropical storms and one typhoon passed close enough to Lamotrek, Elato, and Satawal for their effects to be felt. In May of 1958 these islands were hit by the full force of a typhoon with winds in excess of 100 knots. Severely destructive typhoons were noted by Europeans in 1907, 1845, and 1815 (Krämer 1937:3; Joseph and Murray 1951:28). On Lamotrek in 1962 the effects of the 1958 typhoon were still noticeable. It was only after this length of time that sufficient coconuts were again available for making copra and enough breadfruit was harvested so that some of it could be preserved. If an individual coral island were subject to such storms more often than once every three or four years, the island would be virtually uninhabitable. The abandonment of settlements on Sorol and Lamaliur atolls, as well as Pugue and Falaite islands, can all be traced to the effects of typhoons.

FLORA

Because of the heavy rainfall in the Western Carolines coral island vegetation is lush. Uninhabited and uncleared areas are generally covered by near "jungle" growth. The total number of plant species involved, however, is not great, and many of these have been introduced by man. Stone has enumerated 94 species

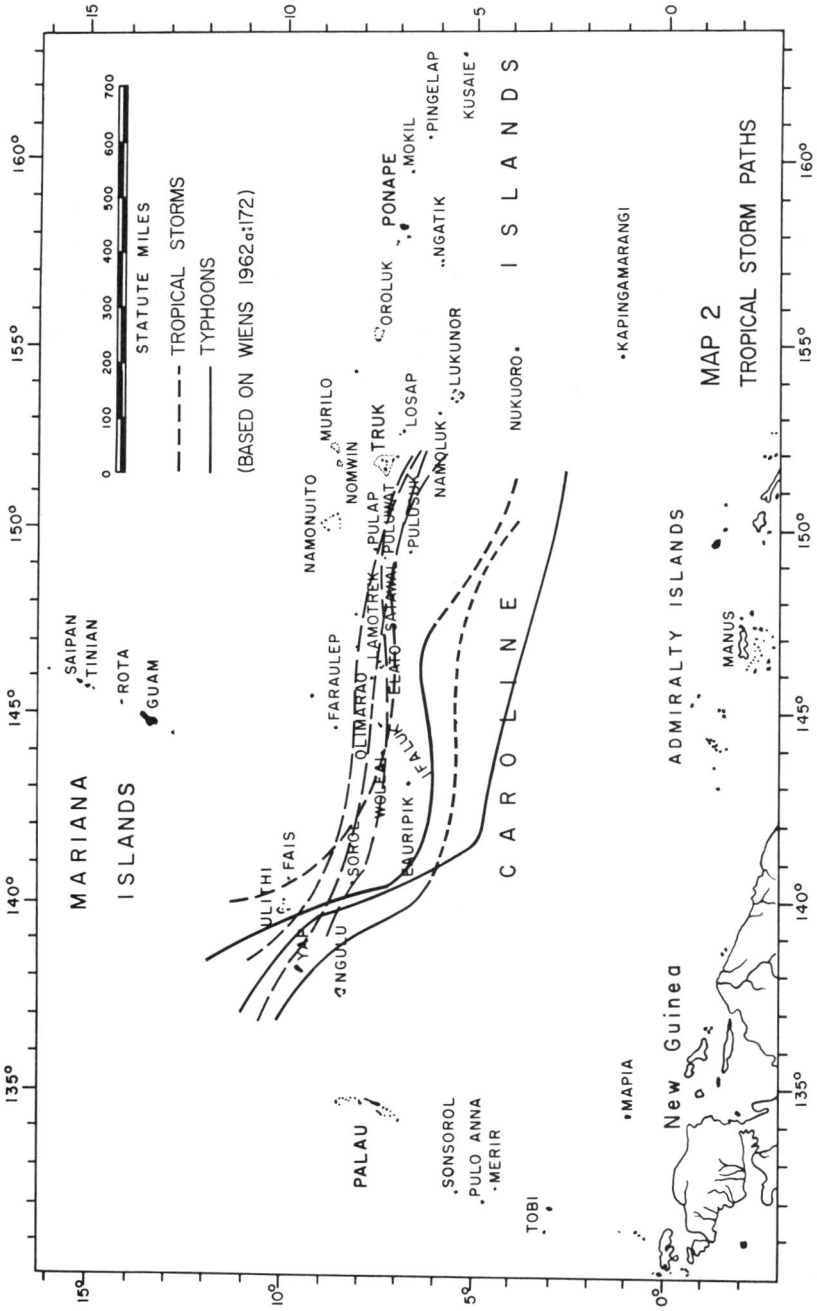

MAP 2

TROPICAL STORM PATHS

Plate 3. Part of the interior swampy area where taro is intensively cultivated.

for Namonuito Atoll, and of these, he states (1959:89), "about 52 can be reasonably construed as indigenous; of the remaining 42 species, 22 are clearly introduced food or ornamental plants; the remaining 20 species are presumably accidental introductions and weeds." It seems reasonable to assume that most of the Western Caroline coral islands are very similar to Namonuito in total number of species present, although some of the smaller and uninhabited islands undoubtedly have fewer.

Coral island vegetation usually is distributed in two or more zones. The first is a strand forest, close to the beach, composed of small trees, such as *Morinda* and *Cordia,* small shrubs and vines, but predominantly introduced coconut palms, shrubs, and flowers. Stone (1959:89) states that inland from this zone on Namonuito the original flora was mainly *Pisonia.* Today, on most islands, one finds cultivated a great deal of coconut, banana, pandanus, breadfruit, *Crataeva,* arrowroot, sweet potato, sugar cane, and tobacco. Any interior swamp is planted in true taro (*Colocasia esculenta*) and false taro (*Cyrtosperma chamissonis*). On the ocean or windward side of an island coconut and breadfruit trees are less dense, bananas and papaya are absent, but pandanus is abundant.

FAUNA

Coral island fauna is also limited to a few species. All of the larger animals have been introduced by man; they include pigs, dogs, cats, chickens, rats, and lizards. Insects abound, and mosquitoes, gnats, flies, scorpions, centipedes, and ants predominate. Terrestrial crabs, of which there are three or more species, and birds, mainly terns, boobies, frigates, and boatswains (Emory 1944: 19), are indigenous and common.

MARINE LIFE

For the purposes of this work sea life can be divided into three categories—reef life, reef and lagoon fishes, and open- or blue-water fishes and mammals.

Nearly all tropical sea life species are numerous in these waters but often localized. On the reef one finds clams (*Tridacna*), cowries, cones, helmets, and trumpets (Abbott 1962). Sea urchins, lobsters, octopus, and morays are also found along the reef. The numerous species of reef fish include sheepshead, parrots, triggers, bass, jewfish, porgies, butterflies, sculpin, puffers, snappers, wrasse, and others (Zim and Shoemaker 1956). Sharks, barracuda, and rays are also numerous along the reef but rarely bother atoll inhabitants.

Open ocean or blue-water fishes in this area of the Western Carolines include sharks, bonito, wahoo, mackerel, dolphin, tuna, sailfish, marlin, and flying fish (La Monte 1952). Whales and porpoises are often sighted. Around some of the atolls turtles are numerous in certain seasons and present throughout the rest of the

Plate 4. Young children gathering sea urchins on the reef on the ocean side of Lamotrek Island.

year. The three species found in the region are the green sea turtle, the hawksbill, and the leatherback (Halstead 1959:132-33).

LAMOTREK, ELATO, AND SATAWAL

Lamotrek, Elato, and Satawal are coral islands which conform to the general descriptions above. The individual characteristics of each should be noted, however, so that some idea may be had of the productive possibilities of each.

Land Area

Lamotrek, Pugue, and Falaite are the three islands which make up Lamotrek Atoll (Map 3). Of the three only Lamotrek is at present inhabited. This island is 4,100 feet long and 2,500 feet wide at its point of greatest width; however, its average width is only 1,650 feet. The total land area of this island is 154 acres or 0.24 square miles. The interior swampy area (Map 9) covers approximately 38 per cent of the total land area, or 58 acres. Pugue is approximately 1,950 feet long and has an average width of 750 feet for a total of 33.3 acres, while Falaite is some 1,100 feet long

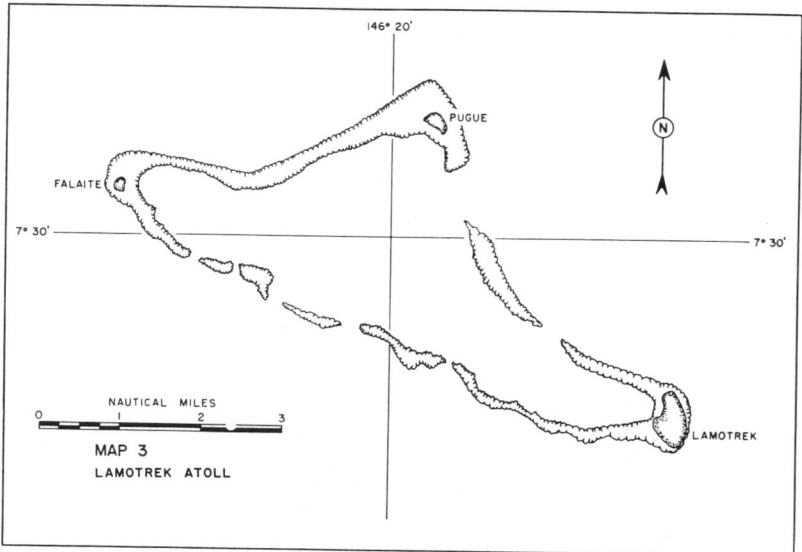

MAP 3
LAMOTREK ATOLL

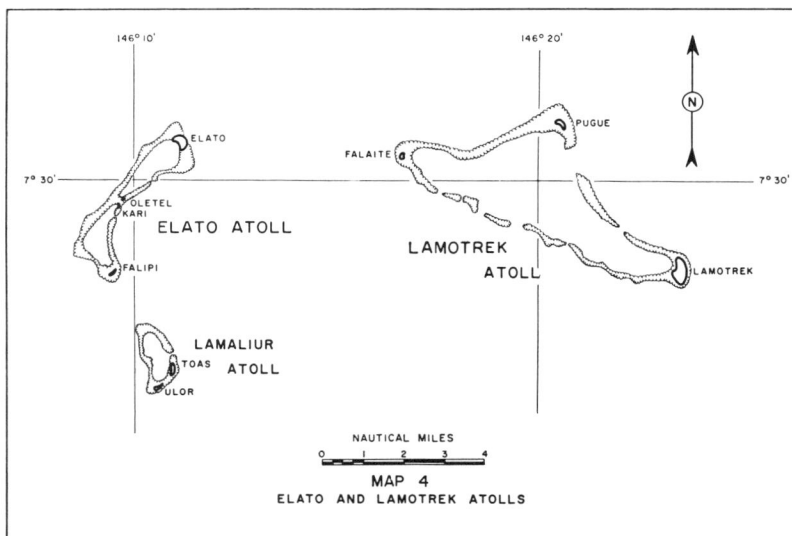

NAUTICAL MILES

MAP 4
ELATO AND LAMOTREK ATOLLS

and averages 650 feet across, thus containing about 16 acres. Each of the three islands has a well-developed fresh-water lens since each is above the minimum size established by Tracy, Abbott, and Arnow (1961:35).

No firsthand measurements were made by this writer on Elato or Satawal, but their areas were computed from U.S. Hydrographic Office charts. Elato Island (U.S.H.O. chart 6042) was found to be approximately 2,800 feet long and averaged 1,245 feet in width. Its total area is 83 acres or 0.13 square miles. There are three other islets on Elato Atoll but only one is more than 300 feet long (Map 4); Falipi is about six acres in area.

There are two islets of significant size in Lamaliur Atoll (occasionally called South Elato Atoll). Toas Island is about 29.4 acres and Ulor Island is some 22 acres in area. The total land area for Elato and Lamaliur atolls together is approximately 0.22 square miles or 141 acres.

Satawal (U.S.H.O. chart 5425) is a single raised coral island 5,250 feet long and on an average 2,050 feet wide. This is approximately 0.39 square miles or 245 acres.

There are two other atolls nearby which, at present, support no

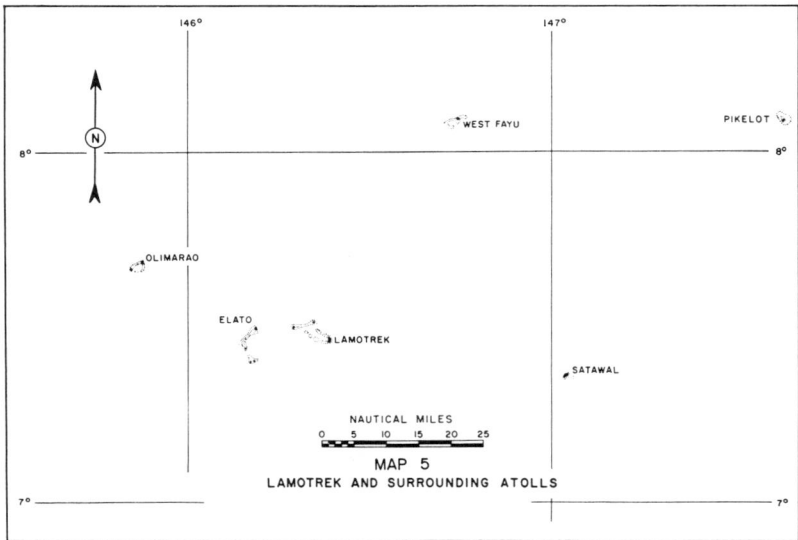

MAP 5
LAMOTREK AND SURROUNDING ATOLLS

permanent populations. These are Olimarao Atoll, frequented by the people of both Lamotrek and Elato; and Pikhailo (West Fayu), often used by the residents of Satawal. The raised coral island of Pikh (Pikelot) is occasionally used by the Satawalese (Map 5). Olimarao Island is 29 acres in area. Pikhailo and Pikh are extremely small islands and are thus not used for agriculture.

Thus, the land area available to the people of Lamotrek and Elato totals 373 acres, while the population of Satawal is confined to about 250 acres.

Reefs and Lagoons

Lamotrek Atoll has some 18 linear miles of reef, which varies in average width from 800 to 1,200 feet. There are two passes on its north side and five on the south which are navigable by canoes. A small winding pass near the south end of Lamotrek Island it-self can be used by canoes during calm weather and at high tide. The lagoon at Lamotrek covers an area of approximately nine square miles.

The reef at Elato has a total lineal run of about ten miles, with an additional four miles at Lamaliur. The lagoon area of Elato and

Lamaliur combined is only about two square miles. The two lagoons of Elato and the one of Lamaliur each has a single pass through the reef.

Satawal Island, being a single raised coral island, does not have the extensive reef development of an atoll. The reef fronting and backing the island totals only two miles in length. Pikhailo Atoll has six miles of reef and one and a half square miles of lagoon.

The People

As in most areas of the Pacific, the population of the islands in the Western Carolines decreased sharply following European discovery. It is often difficult to determine the exact proportions of this depopulation since many of the early estimates of numbers of inhabitants were, undoubtably, inaccurate. Usually the high volcanic islands felt the effects of diseases introduced by Europeans and forced labor more than' outlying coral islands. Yap, for example, has been estimated to have had, at the peak of its indigenous occupation, a population more than three times as large as at present (Wiens 1962b:100). The coral islands were subject to the same depopulating factors as the high islands, but less persistently. On the other hand, coral islands are more susceptible to natural disasters—primarily typhoons and tidal waves—which can cause great damage in a very short time.

Krämer (1937:10) has cited several population estimates for Lamotrek and Elato atolls beginning with one made by Freycinet in 1800. Table I notes this early estimate as well as later figures for a period covering 160 years. It is almost certain that the population

TABLE I. Populations[a]

Island	1800	1890	1909	1930	1958	1962
Lamotrek	2,000	300	220	165	185	201
Elato	1,200	?	?	72	41	49
Satawal	900	200	190	251	285	326
Ulor	180	—	—	—	—	—
Pugue	170	—	—	—	—	—
Falipi	130	—	—	—	—	—
Olimarao	225	—	—	—	—	—

[a] The Japanese government made the 1930 enumeration; the U.S. Trust Territory government made the one in 1958. The 1962 census was taken by the author. These figures from 1800 through 1930 are taken from Krämer (1937) and Damm (1935). The figures for Satawal, 1800 and 1890, are actaully censuses taken in 1819 and 1860.

estimates of 1,800 are much too high (Lessa 1962b:327). The 1890 figure was probably compiled by Lewis and hence should be as reliable a count as the later figures.

In the year 1800, Ulor and Falipi at Elato, Pugue at Lamotrek, and Olimarao Atoll were all inhabited. Graves and remains of house sites on Olimarao and Pugue attest to this fact. Traditional knowledge on Lamotrek and Elato indicates that Toas and Falaite were also once inhabited. By 1890, however, all of these smaller islands were devoid of permanent settlements. Lamotrekan stories relate that the typhoon which struck sometime around 1815 resulted in numerous deaths and the subsequent abandonment of the islands. The survivors either moved to the larger islands within these atolls or migrated to other surrounding islands able to support them. Two hundred such migrants traveled as far as Saipan in the Marianas (Emerick 1958:220). The descendants of these Carolinians, and approximately. 1,000 later Carolinian migrants, are still living on Saipan (Spoehr 1954:326-71).

Even if the early figures are taken as overestimates they suggest that these islands, as well as coral islands in other areas of the Pacific, are capable of supporting dense populations (Wiens 1962b: 93-94). Any coral island which possesses a completely developed fresh-water lens seems capable of sustaining a permanent population.

The decline in population from 1800 through the end of World War II was caused not only by typhoons and other natural disasters but also by diseases introduced with the arrival of foreign powers. The people of Lamotrek recall numerous deaths during the influenza epidemic of 1918 and many others from dysentery, pneumonia, and tuberculosis during the period of Japanese administration. Lessa and Myers (1962) have suggested that the introduction of gonorrhea, and its resultant sterility, was a major factor in the decline in population on the atoll of Ulithi during these same years. Similar reasons for depopulation probably can be proposed for Lamotrek.

Today all of the coral islands of the Western Carolines have populations which are rapidly increasing. As a result, a large proportion of the population is below 16 years of age. Table II gives an age and sex distribution of the populations on Lamotrek and Elato. The figures show that on Lamotrek nearly 43 per cent of the residents are 16 years of age and below; Elato has just under

TABLE II. Populations by Age and Sex

| Island | Adults | | Children (16/under) | | Total |
	Male	Female	Male	Female	
Lamotrek	56	59	43	43	201
Elato	10	17	12	10	49

45 per cent of its population in this category. Illness, primarily pneumonia and amoebic dysentery, is still a factor in limiting population size, but not of such magnitude as to lead to a reduction in total numbers.

3

Kinship and Political Organization

This chapter, as well as the two to follow, will describe the major organizational characteristics of Lamotrekan society. An understanding of organization on the island level is necessary before discussing inter-island ties, since the latter are often extensions of the former. Kinship and political units on Lamotrek are most easily delineated through examining the system of inheritance and control of property.

Goodenough (1951:65-66) delineated five kinds of kin groups on Romonum in the Truk Islands: sib, subsib, ramage, lineage, and descent line. Four similar kinds of groups will be discussed in connection with Lamotrek. I shall call them (using terminology more widely accepted) clan, subclan, lineage, and descent line. A full understanding of both kinship and political organization will also require an examination of marriage, adoption, and the division of the island into districts. Chapter 4 will relate these groupings to the actual exploitation of the environment.

THE CLAN

The largest unit of kinship on Lamotrek is the named matriclan (*hailang*). There are eight of these on Lamotrek, seven of which are traditionally recognized as indigenous to the island. Hofalu, the eighth, is said to be a recent migrant from Satawal. Most of the clans in the Western Caroline atolls are represented on more than one island. There is often a long traditional history associated with a clan, but it is unusual for clan members to be able to trace genealogies back more than seven generations. Within the larger clans, then, it is rarely possible for all its branches on even a single island to be able to trace descent from a common ancestor. The clan name itself may be the only tangible evidence of kinship not only between residents of Lamotrek and visitors from distant atolls of the Western Carolines, but also between different branches of the clan on Lamotrek itself.

Fundamental to the definition of a clan is the rule of exogamy. Nevertheless, because of the inability of clan mates to trace accurate descent in depth, and the limitations imposed on the selection of a spouse by a small population which is subdivided into several exogamous groups, intraclan marriage does occur between certain subdivisions of Mòngalìfach clan. The 1962-63 clan membership on Lamotrek is given in Table III, and, as this table indicates, 50 per

TABLE III. Clan Membership by Sex

Clan	M	F	Clan	M	F
Mòngalìfach	48	54	Hofalu	11	5
Saufalacheg	12	18	Rakh	4	2
Hatamang	4	3	Gailangùwoleai	6	1
Sauwel	13	20	Saur	0	0

cent of the population belongs to Mòngalìfach; each of three other clans has a membership of less than ten individuals, while Saur, a traditional clan of the island, is now extinct. These factors, as well as others related to Mòngalìfach intraclan marriage, will be considered in detail later in this chapter.

The clans of Lamotrek are status ranked. Informants claim that the ranking reflects the order in which these kin groups settled the island; those which have the highest rank are the ones which have been on the island for the longest period of time. The rank of each is as follows: (1) Mòngalìfach, (2) Saufalacheg, (3) Hatamang, (4) Saur, (5) Sauwel, (6) Rakh, (7) Gailangùwoleai. Hofalu, the recent arrival, has no land on the island in its name and is administered through a lineage of Mòngalìfach; hence it is not included in the ranking. This fact may provide some insight into more fundamental reasons for status differences.

The clan is the largest land-holding unit on an island. In principle, the land of a clan is held in common by all members, but in practice, with the exception of those instances where clan membership is very small, this is true in only the loosest sense. If a clan mate, especially one visiting from another island, is in need of food, he can claim use rights to the land of other clan members. However, unless he is able to trace some closer relationship than simply common clan affiliation, he cannot claim inheritance rights to such land until all other individuals with possible rights to the land have been eliminated. This would include not only more closely related clan mates from other islands, but also individuals of other clans who might have adoptive, patrilateral, or gift ties to the land. Thus, as a nonlocalized group the clan holds an estate in common more in principle than in fact. The three clans of highest rank—Mòngalïfach, Saufalacheg, and Hatamang—are chiefly clans. Map 6 shows that by far the majority of Lamotrek land is controlled by these three clans and that the clan of the paramount chief—Mòngalïfach—has larger holdings than either Saufalacheg or Hatamang. Today there is no one-to-one correlation between status and land area controlled. Nevertheless, such may have been the case in the past. Although Map 6 indicates that Hatamang has larger land holdings than does second-ranking Saufalacheg, and Map 7 points out that the land of Sauwel, a nonchiefly clan, is equal in area to that of Saufalacheg, there is clear evidence that both these clans now possess plots received as gifts from lineages of Mòngalïfach.

First, in the case of Hatamang, all of its northern holdings were placed under the authority of this clan when a Mòngalïfach lineage became a controlling faction within Hatamang clan. The means by which this occurred will be discussed later, when adoption is described. Second, as far as Sauwel is concerned its two southernmost holdings (which are among its largest) were received as gifts from Mòngalïfach. These two parcels, as well as some others, were given to Sauwel by a Mòngalïfach lineage which was no longer able to exploit them because of a shortage of manpower within its own ranks. Sauwel was the recipient of the gifts because of traditional, and recently contracted, marriage ties to this Mòngalïfach lineage. Figure 1, which diagrams the significant genealogy of Sauwel clan on Lamotrek, lists Laigorich in the second descending generation. This woman married Itilamorao, a Mòngalïfach man, who passed

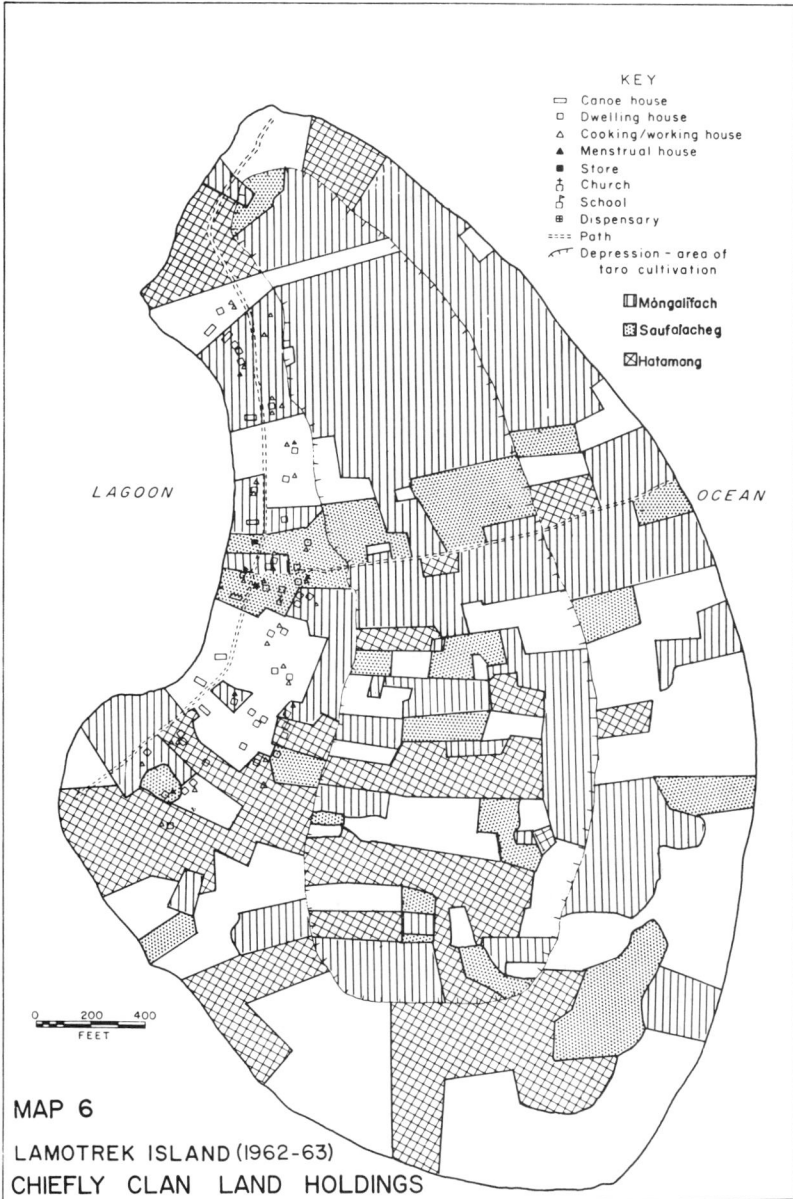

KEY

⊏⊐ Canoe house
▢ Dwelling house
△ Cooking/working house
▲ Menstrual house
■ Store
⛪ Church
🏠 School
⊞ Dispensary
⣿ Path
⌒ Depression – area of
    taro cultivation

▨ Móngalǐfach
▨ Saufalacheg
▨ Hatamang

LAGOON   OCEAN

0   200   400
FEET

MAP 6

LAMOTREK ISLAND (1962-63)
CHIEFLY CLAN LAND HOLDINGS

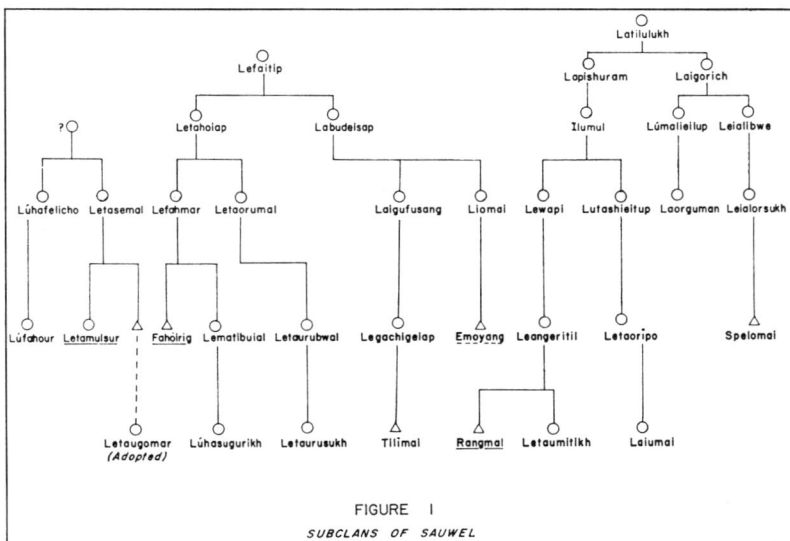

FIGURE   I

SUBCLANS OF SAUWEL

one of the above land parcels of his clan on to his own children, hence on to Sauwel clan. Lefaioup (Figure 2), a woman who is now the paramount chief of Lamotrek, is the sole surviving descendant of Itilamorao's lineage. When a classificatory brother of her's came from Satawal and married a Sauwel woman the ties between the two clans were strengthened. Lefaioup furthered them yet more by giving Sauwel the rest of the mentioned land holdings. Similar transactions among other clans and lineages have led to the widespread redistribution of property as an adjustment to the effects of depopulation and lineage extinction. One might assume, therefore, that in the past the status ranking of a clan was a more direct reflection of the amount of land controlled by that clan.

The political affairs of clans and of the island are organized in the following scheme of roles: (1) the *tamol* (chief), who is the oldest male of the most senior lineage and the appropriate subclan of a chiefly clan; (2) the *tela* (trans., "adze," whom I shall call "subchief"), who is the immediate successor-designate of the chief, usually his younger brother, and/or the senior man of any other lineage of the chief's clan; (3) the *ochang*, the elder men of Saur clan, who have the responsibility of relaying and/or carrying out

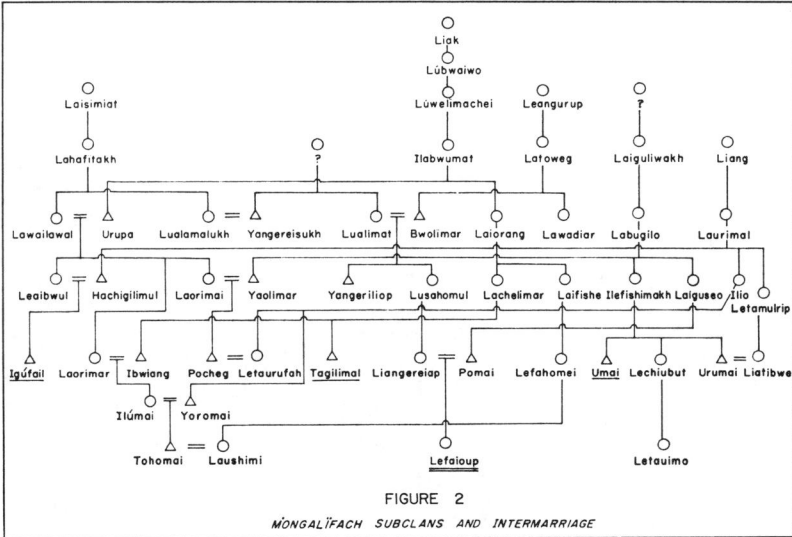

FIGURE 2

MONGALÏFACH SUBCLANS AND INTERMARRIAGE

the directives of the chiefs (primarily the Mòngalïfach chief); and (4) the *aramat* (people), those individuals of all clan affiliations not occupying one of the above positions.

Even though Saur clan is now extinct on the island, the responsibilities of *ochang* have not been transferred to another clan. Instead, those individuals of any clan affiliation who reside on or control Saur land are obligated to carry out Saur functions. At the present time, this includes individuals of both Rakh and Mòngalïfach clans, who are living on the land because of patrilateral relationship to deceased Saur members.

The nonchiefly clans are allowed representation in political decision-making via their most senior male member. These individuals, whose power is theoretically less than that of a *tamol* or *tela,* are called *telalïhailang* (adze of the clan). Island-wide political decisions are made in the following way. In common matters, such as deciding when a canoe house is to be rethatched, the chief of the clan which owns the house, or the *telalïhailang* if the house belongs to a nonchiefly clan, will inform his clan mates and all others who use the structure that the repair is necessary. He will establish a date for the work, so that it does not interfere with some other

Plate 5. Men rethatching Leibwul canoe house.

public function, and tell the clans who use the structure how much thatch each is to contribute. This chief will then inform the other clan chiefs of the work—or the *telalihailang* will first inform the chief of his district (to be discussed later) and the latter will inform the other chiefs. If there is no disagreement about the date word will be passed on to the men of all clans and districts via the *tela* and *ochang*. The men of the island, representing all clans and lineages, will then assemble on the chosen date to contribute labor to the task.

For matters of greater importance, where there may be disagreement concerning the proper course of action, a meeting will usually be called of the men of the island. Decisions which warrant this action range from those determining the proper time for carrying out a particular ceremony to those organizing inter-island activities or local affairs vis-à-vis foreign administrative suggestions. In such cases the three clan chiefs will confer and establish a date for the meeting. They will inform the men of the clans and districts in the usual way via their *tela* and *ochang*, who will often tell the men in the evening, when they have gathered to drink palm wine at the various canoe houses. When the meeting convenes the senior chief will either present the problem or waive this duty to one of the other chiefs. After the opening remarks each of the remaining clan chiefs will discuss his position, then call on the next senior men to state their feelings; these will include the *tela*, *ochang*, and *telalïhailang*. Each of these individuals will either comment on his position or, if he has none, pass without discussion. Any man of lesser status, save in the face of violent feelings, would leave his representation to one of the senior clan or lineage heads. At the

Plate 6. A drinking group at Urieitakh canoe house.

end of the meeting a decision depends on implied unanimity of opinion. If any disagreement remained such a decision would be postponed until a later meeting; thus, ample time is given for tempers to cool (if the argument has been heated) and for the general public opinion to express itself, which any single individual or kin group would find difficult to oppose.

Once each year, at present in January, a general meeting of the entire adult population is called by the paramount chief (*tamolü-falu*). At this time any individual may express grievances or suggest activities for the coming year. I have no evidence about the origin of this meeting, but it seems to have been held with some consistency at least since German times. The order of discussion is much as it was above, but, in addition, the women may voice their feelings, in order of their seniority, after the men. The meeting I attended in January of 1963 was held in the shade of Kulong canoe house (Map 9:E). The women seated themselves toward the rear and along the sides of the structure, apart from the men. The discussion progressed slowly among the men and there were no outstanding suggestions made concerning past or forthcoming activities. The temper changed, though, as the women began to enter the discussion. Lefaioup, the paramount chief of Lamotrek (Figure 2), is a woman and holds this position as the sole survivor of her subclan. She withheld comments until all the men had finished, then expressed herself both as a woman and a chief. She spoke in a normal tone of voice, which was inaudible to those sitting more than a few feet from her; thus her words had to be repeated by a nearby woman so that all could hear. She first said that, as a woman, she realized that she was not as intelligent as a man, but she did wish to make an observation. As of late, she said, the men had been drinking too much and working too little. She felt a change was needed. Her position was supported by the senior woman of Sauwel clan, who added that there were better things to do for the men than simply to come home drunk at night and argue with their wives. This commentary took the men somewhat by surprise, but the Saufalacheg chief met the occasion with a counterattack. He said that comparisons of work output would show that the women were little better. It is quite obvious, he held, that the women spend most of their time in the afternoon either gossiping or sleeping (it might be added that this chief was unmarried). Lefaioup replied that, indeed, a comparison should be made and that it would show all

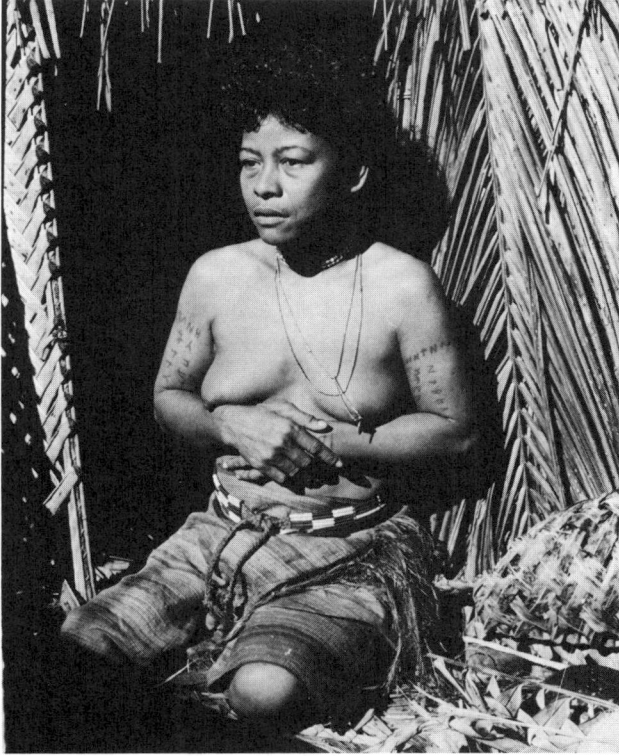

Plate 7. Lefaioup, the paramount chief (*tamolüfalu*) of Lamotrek.

the people well fed, as a result of the women's agricultural efforts, but the small amount of copra sold during the last visit of the trading ship amply demonstrated the indolence of the men. Therefore, Lefaioup continued, she was taking her share of the copra funds, which she receives as paramount chief from those individuals who work public lands (which are those land areas found in neighboring uninhabited atolls) and spending it not on the whole community, as is traditional, but solely for the benefit of the women and children. None of the men replied to this.

The conduct of the two meetings mentioned above illustrates several things. First, all clans and their major subdivisions, whether chiefly or not, have representation at interclan meetings. Second, it is usual for agreement to be unanimous. This is achieved when one side or the other backs down in the face of a stronger position or in the face of public opinion. Third, although a woman's position is traditionally restricted in the field of politics, it is obvious that she wields power both through the senior male representing her clan or lineage, with whom she will often consult, and by voicing her position openly at the proper time, such as the annual meeting. And last, the position of paramount chief is not simply ceremonial. Even though the present occupant is a woman, her decisions, although possibly disliked by many of the men, are defended as being within her rights and accepted as such. Informants stated that in the past, when men occupied the position of paramount chief, power was even more concentrated and there was less consultation among the chiefs or other elders before a decision was made. Indeed, some men felt that much of the indecisiveness concerning present-day political action was due to the decreasing influence of the paramount chief. Evidence to be discussed later will amplify upon this and further delineate the roles of chiefs.

THE SUBCLAN

There are no named kin groups below clan level. Nevertheless there are significant and recognized subdivisions of the clan which are important genealogically and politically. Figure 1 diagrams the important genealogical history of Sauwel, the largest nonchiefly clan on Lamotrek, while Figure 2 depicts Mòngalïfach, the largest and most important chiefly *hailang*. Although it is usually not possible to trace subclan descent back to a common named ancestor, common descent, in more general terms, is recognized as the binding factor for such a group. When descent is not readily traceable, an ancestor of one line will simply be described as *bwisübwis* to one in the other line of the subclan. In view of the generation type of terminology common to these islands, as shown in Figure 5, such a sibling relationship could refer to an individual in one of a number of collateral lines. In the case of Mòngalïfach (Figure 2), for example, informants remember that a sibling relationship existed between Leangùrup and the mother of Laiguliwakh, although the exact characteristics of this relationship are not known. Similarly, Leangùrup is known to have been related to Lüwelïmachei, but these ties are even less distinct and cannot be definitely assigned to the same generation. These women, therefore, were *bwisübwis* (trans., "sisters of sisters") and the three branches they represent are assigned to a single subclan. On the other hand, no closer relationship than simply clan name is recalled for the branches of Laisimiat, the mother of Lualimat, and Liang; thus, they are of separate subclans. Sauwel (Figure 1) is more clearly divided into three separate groups, originating with Latilulukh, Lefaitip, and the mother of Letasemal. The subclan, then, can be defined as that kin group which extends to the limits of any kind of genealogical reckoning. A distinction based solely on such imprecisely remembered relationships might seem unduly vague. Nevertheless, these descent groups are manifest in the area of rights and obligations. In practice, the subclan can best be further defined as (1) the largest kin group in which an orderly transmission of property by matri-inheritance from one generation to the next occurs, and (2) the largest kin group to which political positions are normally restricted.

Sauwel, with its constituent subclans, can best be used to illustrate the factor of restricted inheritance of property. This clan, as shown in Figure 1, is clearly divided into three branches, each of which controls specific land parcels on the island. Letamulsur is the sole living member of her subclan and since her brother's death she has had to act as head of it. Letamulsur insists that although Sauwel is one clan and thus all of its members are related, no other Sauwel member on Lamotrek has rights to her land; their relationship is too distant. For example, traditional history says that one of these branches originated on Woleai while the second came to Lamotrek from Kusaie via Ifaluk. Letamulsur insists that she will pass her land on to Letaugomar, her brother's adopted daughter, who is now living with Letamulsur. All other Sauwel representatives on the island recognize Letamulsur's right to dispose of her property in this way just as they insist that each of the other subclans has no rights to their respective holdings. Letaugomar herself is Sauwel, but from Ulithi and in no closer relationship to Letamulsur than any other Sauwel resident of Lamotrek. Her right to the land is justified as a gift from her adoptive patrilateral clan.

Specific political positions under normal circumstances cannot cross subclan boundaries either. The situation, as it exists today, in Mòngalïfach clan can best illustrate this. Mòngalïfach (Figure 2) is divided into four subclans which are much more difficult to disentangle, owing to complications of marriage and residence, than

Plate 8. Tagilimal, chief of the northern district and acting chief of Móngalïfach.

was the case with Sauwel. The question of property transfer is
much the same among these units as it was above. The four subclans are branches stemming from the mother of Lualimat, Liak
and her *bwisübwis*, who ties Leangürup to this line, Liang, and
Laisimiat. For analytic purposes I shall call these subclans M-I,
M-II, M-III, and M-IV, respectively. The paramount chief or *tamolüfalu* (chief of the island) of Lamotrek is Lefaioup. There are
several men on the island, older by generation as well as years, who
could head Móngalïfach if the title of *tamolüfalu* could cross subclan boundaries. Since that is not possible, Lefaioup, although a
woman, must fill the position, and has done so since coming of age.
The administration of the position is further complicated by the
fact that Lefaioup is so crippled as to be unable to walk without
the aid of a crutch, although she is still a young woman. Because of

her physical condition, she has appointed Tagilimal, the oldest man of M-II, to act in her place in carrying out the day-to-day functions of the paramount chieftainship. Most people recognize, though, that this is a temporary solution to the problem of the *tamolüfalu*, for if Tagilimal had a real genealogical right to the position he would naturally have taken precedence over Lafaioup in the first place. As it is, however, there is even some dispute over whether Lefaioup should have chosen Tagilimal over Umai, who, although younger than the former, is held to outrank him in terms of genealogical status. The culmination of this dispute will probably occur when Lefaioup dies and a new *tamolüfalu* is chosen. M-II may try to press a claim to a position traditionally restricted to M-I on the grounds that all members of M-I who were born on and residents of Lamotrek are dead. More likely, though, because subclan membership is not limited to individuals on this island alone, an M-I individual from a neighboring island will be sought out to assume the chieftainship. This alternative directly concerns inter-island political organization; thus it will be discussed in detail in Chapter 7.

Subclan land holdings are often localized on Lamotrek itself. Map 7 shows that Sauwel's holdings are clustered in three general regions—the north, middle, and south. The northern land belongs to Letamulsur's subclan, the middle to Rangmal's, and the southern plots to Fahóirig. Similarly, Map 8 lists the holdings of M-I, M-II, and M-III. Lefaioup's M-I land predominates in the south. Tagilimal and Umai's M-II land is primarily located in the north, while Yoromai's M-III land is centered in the middle area of the island. M-IV of Igüfail is not included in this discussion even though, genealogically, it is a part of this clan; for realistically and residentially the members of this subclan and its land holdings are under the jurisdiction of the chief of Hatamang clan. This peculiar situation will be considered below as a factor of adoption and marriage. In any case, however, subclans themselves cannot be referred to as localized, for the alternative methods of inheritance lead to a dispersion of personnel in order to activate claims to newly acquired land.

THE LINEAGE

The lineage is the third kind of kin group of Lamotrekan society to be discussed and is probably the most important in day-to-day activities. Lineages are status ranked within subclans just as the

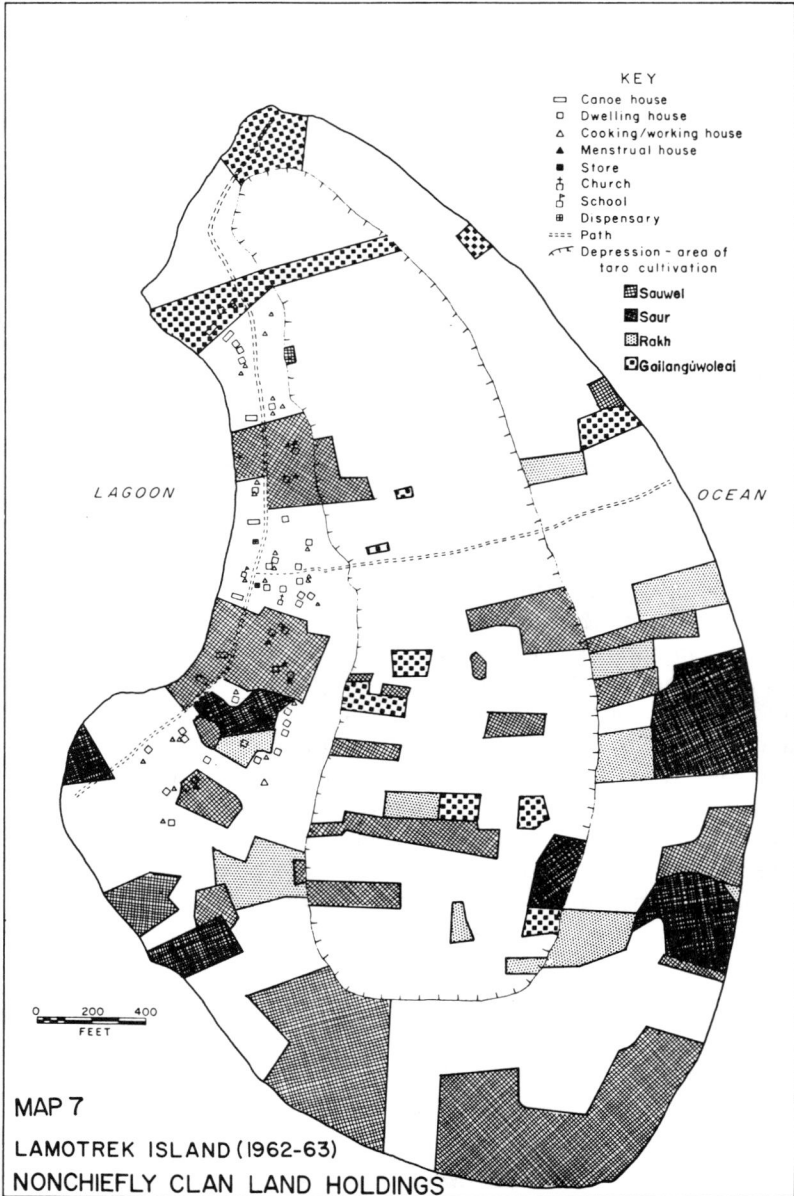

KEY
- ⬚ Canoe house
- ▭ Dwelling house
- △ Cooking/working house
- ▲ Menstrual house
- ■ Store
- ⌂ Church
- ⌂ School
- ⊞ Dispensary
- ==== Path
- ⌄⌄ Depression – area of taro cultivation

- ⊞ Sauwel
- ◼ Saur
- ▦ Rakh
- ⬓ Gailangúwoleai

LAGOON

OCEAN

0   200   400
FEET

MAP 7

LAMOTREK ISLAND (1962-63)
NONCHIEFLY CLAN LAND HOLDINGS

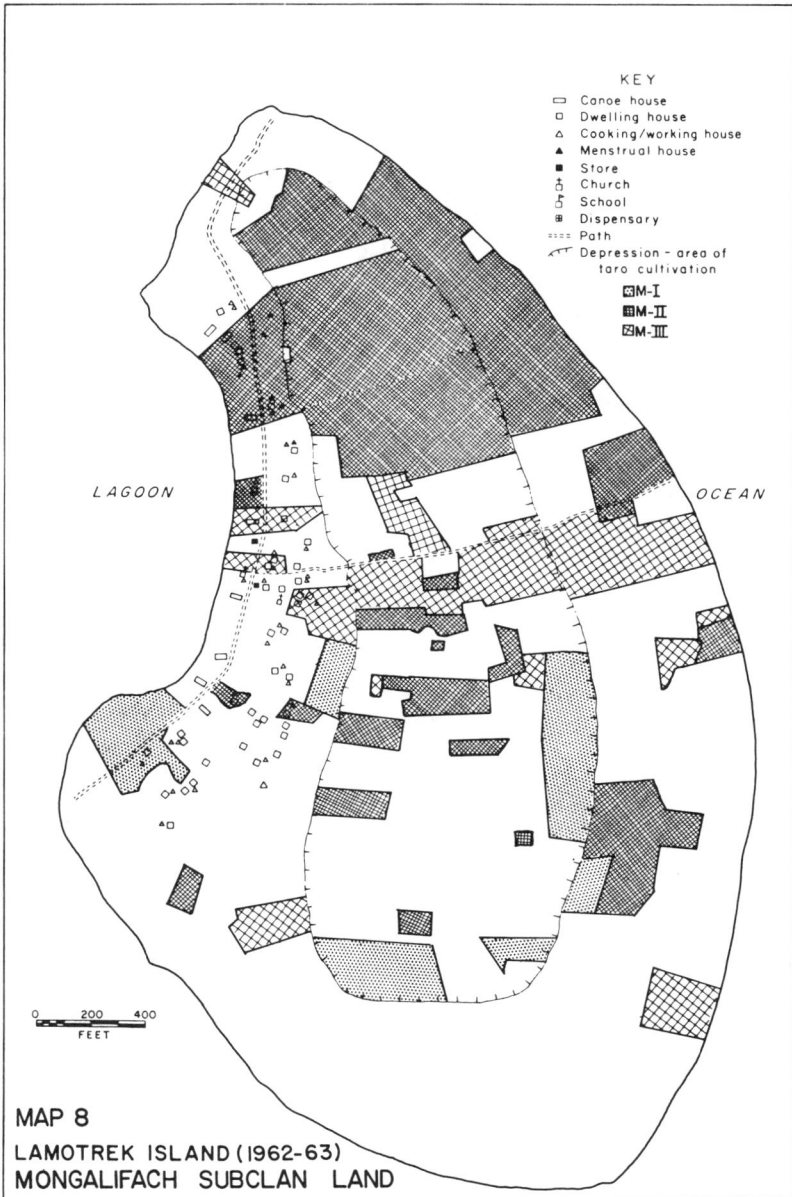

KEY
☐ Canoe house
☐ Dwelling house
△ Cooking/working house
▲ Menstrual house
■ Store
⌐ Church
⌐ School
⊞ Dispensary
:::: Path
⌃⌃ Depression - area of
     taro cultivation
▦ M-I
▦ M-II
▨ M-III

LAGOON

OCEAN

0   200   400
FEET

MAP 8
LAMOTREK ISLAND (1962-63)
MONGALIFACH SUBCLAN LAND

latter are ranked within clans. The status of a particular lineage when compared to another of the same subclan depends on the seniority of the women from whom they trace their descent. A lineage is always traced from a known ancestor and her status when compared to any siblings of the same generation is known, so that respective lineages which originated with these women are ranked as they themselves were. Subclan M-II, for example, is made up of three lineages which originated with Lùwelïmachei, Leangùrup, and the mother of Laiguliwakh. Leangùrup is thought to have been senior to Lùwelïmachei; thus, Umai today would outrank Tagilimal. Lefaioup, as mentioned above, however, chose the latter as her representative and her decision was not disputed. Eventually, this ranking will mean that primary positions will be passed on in the lineage of Umai, and only secondarily in that of Tagilimal.

The case of Saufalacheg, the second-ranking chiefly clan, can be cited to further clarify lineage ranking. Figure 3 is a diagram of the descent of the component lineages of this clan. The three lineages of Saufalacheg are all members of the same subclan; thus they not only have a common traditional history, but also Saufalacheg land and titles pass freely from one of its lineages to another. The chief

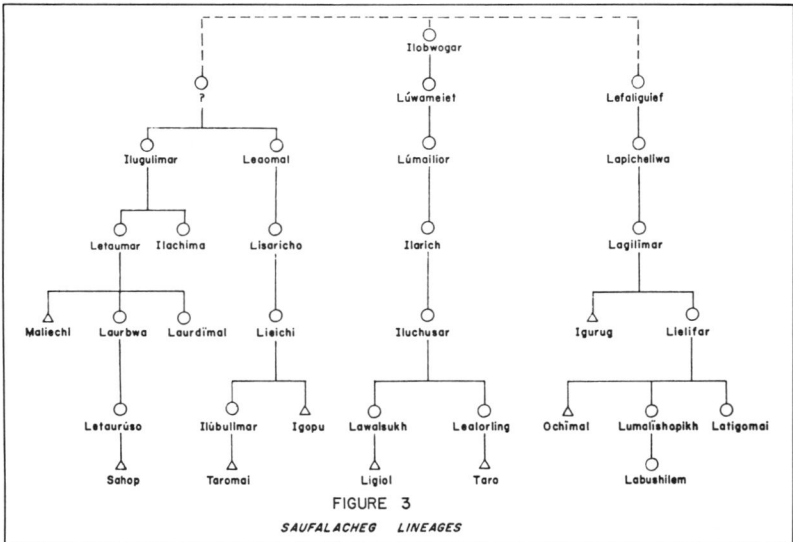

FIGURE 3

SAUFALACHEG   LINEAGES

of Saufalacheg is Ligiol; he assumed this position at the death of Ochïmal. At that time, Laurbwa was the senior woman or *shab-wuttugofaielïbwogat* (old woman of the land) of the clan. Figure 3 shows that each of these individuals is of a different lineage of the clan. The status ranking within Saufalacheg is said to be as follows. The lineage originating with the mother of Ilugulimar and Leaomal is the most senior, and the descent line, which is merely a lineage branch (Goodenough 1951:35), of Ilugulimar has precedence over that of Leaomal. Lefaliguief's lineage is ranked second and that of Ilobwogar last. According to this ranking Sahop, a direct descendant of Ilugulimar, should have assumed the chieftainship when Ochïmal died. Neither he nor Taromai did, however, because of their youth: at that time Sahop was about 8 and Taromai 15. As a result, Ligiol was chosen as *tamol* by Laurbwa. He will hold the position until his death, when it may be assumed that it will pass back to Sahop and the lineage he represents.

The difference between this situation and that previously described for Mòngalïfach is illustrative of the difference between

Plate 9. Ligiol, chief of the middle district and of Saufalacheg clan.

subclans and lineages. Within Mòngalìfach, Tagilimal or Umai could not become paramount chief because of a subclan difference; Ligiol can become Saufalacheg chief because of the subclan unity of this *hailang* on Lamotrek. On Elato Island, however, where Mòngalìfach also holds the paramount chieftainship and Saufalacheg a secondary one, at present there is no Saufalacheg *tamol*, because none of the Elatoan residents are of the proper subclan to assume the position.

An individual will usually identify the lineage to which he belongs in one of two ways; he will name the senior man of his lineage as the individual to whom he owes allegiance in work, for example, or, more usually, he will refer to himself as an individual of a particular *bwogat*. Literally, a *bwogat* is a group of land parcels collectively referred to by the name of one of the component plots. In practice, though, a *bwogat* is more than land; it is also the people who live upon and control it. I have chosen to translate *bwogat* as "homestead."

The general pattern of settlement on Lamotrek (Map 9) is typical of neither what is usually meant by a village nor a hamlet. Although the distance from one end of the settlement to the other or between individual houses is not great, this is more a reflection of the restricted size of the island than of an underlying rule of settlement. The primary identification of an individual is with a parcel of land to which he has inheritance rights and upon which he, at some time or other in his life, has resided. In most cases this will be a land parcel controlled by a matrilineage. The dispersed nature of the settlement on Lamotrek suggests residential units more autonomous than would be usual in a village type of settlement primarily because land on which residences are found also has great importance as subsistence agricultural areas. This is a characteristic which would not be commonly understood in the term "village." Individual residences themselves are not accurately described by the term "household," either. A residential plot may have more than one dwelling on it—some may have as many as seven. "Homestead" seems to be a more accurate term when understood as follows:

1. *The homestead is a named plot of land on which one or more dwellings are located, plus associated, contiguous or dispersed, individually named plots which are primarily agricultural, all of which are collectively referred to as the land of X bwogat.* An example

should clarify this point. At the north end of Lamotrek Island is Hapilamahal *bwogat* (Map 9:2). Hapilamahal is specifically the name of the plot of land on the northeast side of the path where no dwellings now stand. The houses of the *bwogat* are found on plots which are named Leibwul, Hafiliang, and Haoshakh. There are also adjoining land parcels called Meiur and Maigurup, plus other plots in other districts of the island, belonging to this homestead. Collectively, they are called Hapilamahal *bwogat*.

2. *A homestead* (bwogat) *is the seat of a lineage.* Since lineages are not named it is easiest to speak of a genealogically related group of people below clan or subclan level as "people of the homestead." *Bwogat*, in meaning, is interchangeably used for both the land and the people who own it. *Bwogatai* can mean "my land" but more frequently "my family," i.e., "my lineage," since no single individual would presume to imply he alone owns the land. On any particular *bwogat* individuals who are not genealogically related (e.g., men living uxorilocally, adopted individuals, etc.) may also be resident, but they would be under the jurisdiction of the *bwogat* matrigroup. When individuals of this category spoke of their *bwogatai*, they would have to clarify whether they were referring to their *bwogat* of origin or residence.

In summary, the settlement of Lamotrek is not in the form of a compact residential village, but rather on dispersed residential-agricultural land parcels which could be termed farmsteads or homesteads. I have chosen the latter designation because of the genealogical relationship of its residents and potential inheritors, most of whom belong to a lineage or descent line and who, in referential conversation, are distinguished from their clan mates by the name of their lineage seat or *bwogat*.

There are 25 functioning homesteads on Lamotrek. Because of depopulation and the problem of lineage and clan extinction, some present-day *bwogat* are made up of land parcels which once were divided into two or more *bwogat*. Similarly, other *bwogat* are no longer the seats of lineages but, because of the scarcity of personnel, are settled and controlled by lineage segments. Table IV, keyed to Map 9, lists the 25 homesteads, the number of residents on each, and their clan affiliation. The table is arranged so that *bwogat* are grouped according to the matriclan (*hailang*) to which they belong. Each *bwogat* has its inhabitants broken down according to the rule of residence followed. Column 1 includes all individuals who are

TABLE IV. Homesteads and Rule of Residence[a]

Bwogat	Matriuxor.	Patrivir.	Adopt.	Other
Móngalïfach clan				
2 Hapilamahal	10	2	2	0
B Leibwul (canoe house)				
3 Olipúpú	8	0	2	0
C Urieitakh (canoe house)				
5 Omaras	5	0	0	0
D Falamara (canoe house)				
7 Hapalam	10	0	1	0
10 Onïsal (Hofalu)	7	0	0	0
13 Sarishe	2	0	2	0
14 Hapilifal	4	0	3	0
F Lugal (canoe house)				
22 Fairochekh	1	5	0	0
Saufalacheg clan				
6 Chiligilafa	7	0	1	0
8 Faligiliau	5	3	3	0
E Kulong (canoe house)				
9 Imúpú	1	3	1	0
18 Leomoi	6	0	0	0
24 Ralumai	2	0	1	0
Hatamang clan				
16 Iaopïl	8	1	0	0
19 Limaraorao	2	1	0	0
21 Onesh	1	2	3	0
G Yapúi (canoe house)				
20 Lugulior	7	0	1	1
25 Peiliwer	4	2	1	0
Sauwel clan				
4 Imuailap	6	0	4	0
11 Leomar	14	0	1	2
12 Sabwaikh	5	0	1	0
23 Leihao	3	1	1	0
Saur clan				
15 Leiho	0	7	1	0
H Hatiwa (canoe house)				
Rakh clan				
17 Iloritur	5	0	3	0
Gailangùwoleai clan				
1 Lechib	8	1	2	0
A Falabwul (canoe house)				

[a] The homesteads have an average of eight residents each; 68 per cent are living matriuxorilocally, 12 per cent patrivirilocally, 17 per cent adopted.

residing matrilocally, their spouses (uxorilocally), and children. Column 2 covers those individuals residing patrilocally, their spouses (virilocally) and children. Column 3 includes residents who have been adopted by members of the *bwogat* and are living on the homestead for this reason. The final column covers all other residents, few in number, who may be living on a particular *bwogat* as unrelated visitors from another island or friends of *bwogat* residents. There are several unmarried young men who sleep in canoe houses rather than in dwelling houses. They are not assigned to a particular house in this table because such men often move from one to another, weekly or even nightly, depending on drinking groups to which they belong, friends with whom they wish to converse, or the use to which a particular canoe house is being put. The canoe houses are listed in the table so that their clan affiliation may be noted.

Some of the *bwogat* listed in Table IV are not, however, lineage seats. Processes which lead to lineage emergence and extinction require that land be periodically redistributed. As a result, some *bwogat* may often be uninhabited or controlled by a descent line which is a lineage segment. By way of example, Figures 1, 2, 3, and

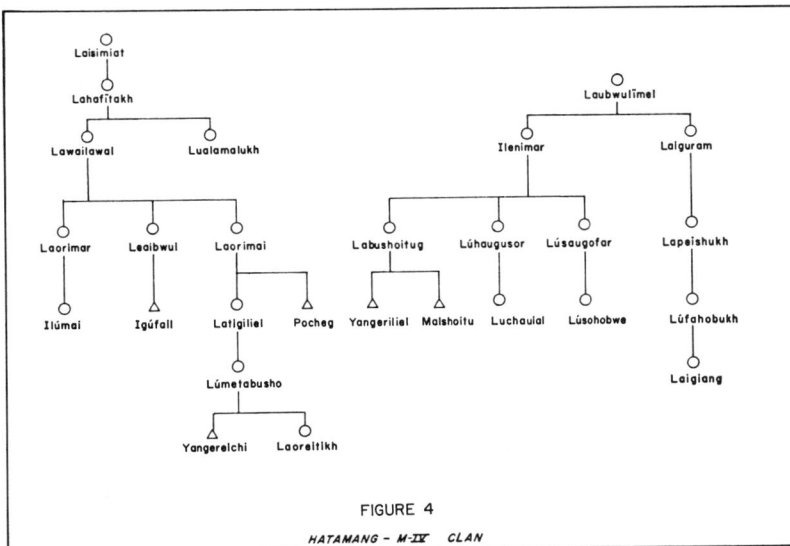

FIGURE 4

HATAMANG - M-II CLAN

Clan	Lineage (or descent line) Head	*Bwogat* Seat
Sauwel	Letamulsur	Imuailap
	Rangmal	Leomar
	(Labuchailem: adopted here)	Sabwaikh
	Fahòirig	Leihao
Mòngalïfach	Lefaioup	Fairochekh
	Umai	Hapilamahal
	(Letalimo)	Hapilifal
	Tagilimal	Olipùpù
	(Letarior)	Omaras
	(Laigiel)	Sarishe
	Yoromai	Hapalam
	(Ileipisemel: patrilateral)	Onïsal (Hofalu)
Saufalacheg	Laurbwa	Leomoi
	(Ileileg: adopted here)	Faligiliau
	(Latigomai)	Ralumai
	Ligiol	Chiligilafa
	(Lealorlukh)	Imùpù
Hatamang	Igùfail	Onesh
	(Ilùsurtil: adopted here)	Limaraorao
	(Ilùmai)	Lugulior
	Malshoitu	Iaopïl
	Yangereichi	Peiliwer

4 are correlated with Table IV in the columns above. Each lineage head is listed opposite the *bwogat* seat of that lineage. In those cases where a homestead is controlled by a descent line the name of the most senior member of the line is noted in parentheses. Descent line *bwogat* are listed immediately following the lineage *bwogat* from which its residents migrated.

Rakh, Gailangùwoleai, and Saur (representatives) are each centered on a single homestead with no clan subdivision.

A new residential group (e.g., descent line) and potential lineage will break away from a mother lineage in the following way: Faligiliau is the original residence of the most senior Saufalacheg lineage. Before acquisition of Leomoi and Ralumai all of the *bwogat* of this clan (conforming to the previously cited rule concerning "localization" of subclans) were localized in the central district of the island. Ilugulimar married Faramel, a Hatamang man, who gave Leomoi to his own children when he died. As will be shown, this type of patrilateral land gift is quite common. In order for Saufalacheg to maintain control of Leomoi a member of Ilugulimar's lineage had to continue to reside upon this land, otherwise the holding would revert to Hatamang. Laurbwa, who is a member of the proper lineage, does reside on Leomoi. Nevertheless, this *bwogat* has not supplanted Faligiliau as the seat of the lineage, for full ownership of it does not rest with Saufalacheg: residual ownership of Leomoi remains with Hatamang. The picture is further complicated by the fact that at present no Saufalacheg people live at Faligiliau. Ileileg is the oldest female on the land and she is Mòngalïfach. She is living here for reasons similar but not identical to those which explain Laurbwa's residence at Leomoi. Ileileg's father was Igopu, a Saufalacheg man. Igopu supposedly did not give Faligiliau to Ileileg but only told her, before he died, that she could continue to live here if she so desired with usufruct rights to the products of the land. Thus, Faligiliau continues to be the seat or "headquarters" of Saufalacheg even though no one from that clan now resides upon it.

In another case, Sarishe *bwogat* came under the control of Mòngalïfach *hailang* when Lachelimar married Yaloitukh, a man of Sauwel. Yaloitukh gave this homestead to his children, and the descendants of these children must continue to reside here or be challenged by Sauwel for active ownership of the land. Here the situation is further complicated by the fact that not Sauwel but Hatamang is the original or residual owner of this *bwogat*. Yaloitukh gained control of the land because he was adopted by a Hatamang woman and moved to this homestead to live with his adoptive parents. Thus, if Mòngalïfach does not maintain residence on Sarishe, it could revert back to Sauwel; if Sauwel does not take up residence the land will return to Hatamang.

In both of the above cases—Leomoi and Sarishe—the descent group resident upon the land must present periodic *paliwen* (payment) to the original owners of the land. The two occasions when *paliwen* is necessary are at the funeral of someone in the residual owner's lineage and when that lineage repairs one of its canoe houses. At a funeral *paliwen* is in the form of trade cloth or woven skirts (*tur*); for the repair of a canoe house several hundred fathoms of sennit twine are given. This gift symbolizes the recognition of the residence group that the donor lineage actually retains residual rights to the land. In summary, a descent line will usually break away from its mother lineage to take up residence on land which it has received as a gift and for which it must pay *paliwen*. And conversely, land which is the seat of a lineage is land for which the residual rights are held and which traditionally has the most senior status among all the land holdings of that lineage. It is conceivable that with the passage of several generations and the extinction of the lineage of residual ownership, *paliwen* may no longer be offered and eventually full ownership might be assumed by the first recipient descent group. With expansion of this group it might break completely away from its mother lineage and assume lineage (or possibly subclan) status itself.

In all of the above instances where a descent line is settled on a *bwogat* other than one which residually belongs to its lineage the homestead was acquired as either a patrilateral or adoptive gift. The breakdown is as follows:

Bwogat	Means of Acquisition	*Paliwen* Given to:
Sabwaikh	Adoption	Mòngalïfach
Hapilifal	?	Saur (inactive)
Omaras	Patrilateral	(M-III)
Sarishe	Patrilateral via adoption	Hatamang
Onïsal	Patrilateral	Mòngalïfach
Leomoi	Patrilateral	Hatamang
Ralumai	Patrilateral	Mòngalïfach

Imùpù and Lugulior are also residences of descent groups but are *bwogat* traditionally belonging to the lineages whose residents are settled there. They have probably been settled because of the proliferation of their respective lineages and the need for additional living space. Thus they could easily develop into independent lineages themselves, if their membership continues to expand during the next few generations. Land received as a patrilateral or adoptive gift cannot be passed into the general holdings of the whole subclan or clan until *paliwen* is no longer given to the residual owner. Usually *paliwen* is only stopped when the lineage having residual ownership becomes extinct. Saur is a case in point; Mòngalïfach can no longer offer *paliwen* to Saur for Hapilifal or Leiho for Saur is now extinct on the island. Leiho, which is the lineage seat of Saur, is settled by Mòngalïfach and Rakh individuals and because of the requirements of the political structure they are looked upon as if they were Saur or at least under Saur jurisdiction.

Kinship terminology (Figure 5) is of a type that makes it easy to accommodate patrilateral and adoptive land gifts. Western Caro-

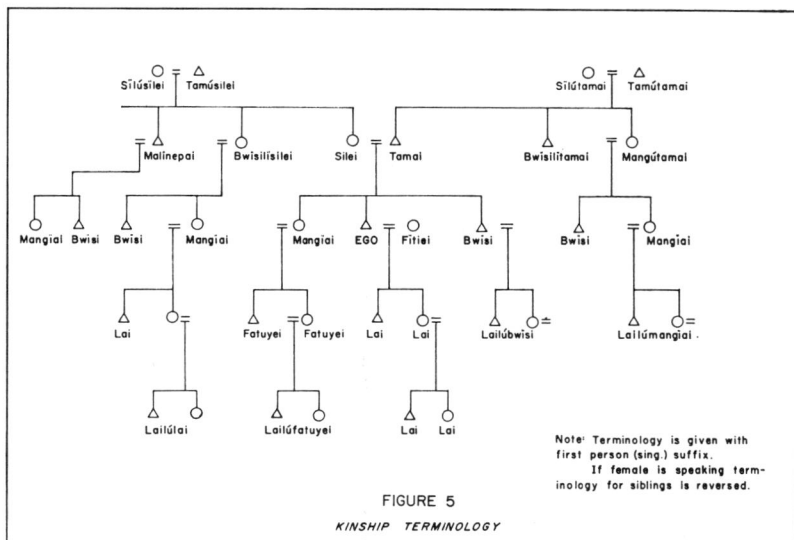

FIGURE 5

KINSHIP TERMINOLOGY

linian atoll terminology places emphasis on generational standing and matrilineal organization—but the latter is apparent only in terms between mother's brother and sister's son (daughter). In ego's own generation there is an extension of terms to matrilateral and patrilateral cognates alike; in the next descending generation, a male ego calls his children and those of his matrilateral female cousins (who are matrilineal inheritors of ego's lineage possessions) by the same terms. Terminology itself does not play a very active part in categorizing individuals; one invariably calls a kinsman by his name and uses a kin term only when specifically asked what relationship exists between them. If this is necessary an informant will most often respond with a simple generational term, e.g., *silei* (my mother), *bwïsi* (my sibling of the same sex), or *lai* (my child). If a specific relationship is demanded he will resort to an exact description, e.g., *sïlùsïlei* (mother of my mother), or *tamùtamai* (father of my father), or *lailùbwïsi* (child of my brother). Ties which are established between more distant matrirelatives or between persons not matrirelatives through patrilateral or adoptive land gifts do not require widespread readjustment of such referential terminology but simply extension of it to additional individuals of the appropriate generation. The acceptance of a patrilateral or adoptive land gift establishes a specific relationship between the recipient lineage and the donor descent group concerned; one characteristic of this is that any member of the donor descent group is prohibited from marrying into the recipient lineage so long as such individuals continue to reside on or recognize ties to the land concerned.

In a small population such as inhabits Lamotrek it is easy to see how natural processes can lead to the extinction of lineages. Disease, accidents, and natural disasters might lead to the disappearance of a lineage or even of a clan in two or three generations. Land redistribution would be necessary because of this as well as because of any increase in the size of other lineages. And in the case of extinction, alternatives to matriliny are necessary if orderly redistribution is to occur. Adoption and patrilateral transmission of property are these alternatives. Patrilateral and adoptive gifts most often transfer land across clan boundaries, and even though these are traditionally recognized ways of transferring property the possibility of interclan dispute over ownership often arises. For example, a donor lineage may question whether the recipient descent group has full or only use rights to the land, and when the donor himself is dead it is often difficult to clear up the exact terms of the patrilateral gift. Disputes which result from situations such as this are seldom resolved. Instead a truce is reached, usually of one generation's duration, in which one side will back down in favor of the other in order to avoid open conflict. Residence itself will be the prime determinant of who is able to maintain his claim. Nevertheless, the fact that one side in the dispute does not actively assert its claim does not mean that when a new alignment of lineage and clan strength occurs, perhaps in a later generation, a renewed claim will not be made.

MARRIAGE AND ADOPTION

The average Lamotrekan male will contract 3.6 marriages during his life and the average female 3.2. In 1963 the high extremes were represented by a man who had been married ten different times and a woman who had had eight different spouses. Such multiple marriages are, or were until recent missionary influence, very common, but polygamy was not. Informants cited one woman still alive on the island who had been co-wife, along with another woman, now dead, to a man during German times. On another occasion joking reference was made to the practice during the 1963 New Year's celebration, when three women performed as *hüfäs* (jokester). One of the women was decorated as a man while the other two appeared in normal dress except that one was padded in simulated pregnancy. The first told the crowd that she was a man of Satawal and the two women were sisters and "his" wives. Other than these two instances, and stories which make reference to sororal polygyny and fraternal polyandry, there is no evidence that such multiple marriages were very common. It was common, however, for men to allow their brothers access to their wives when the husband himself was away from the island for extended periods. "Serial sororal polygyny," though, is still common. That is, several instances were recorded where a man had married a girl, divorced her, and then married the sister of this former wife. Similarly, a number of cases were noted in which a woman had divorced a man to marry his brother.

Nearly all first marriages are arranged by and contracted between the two lineages concerned. Sometime between the ages of 18 and 23 a young man will have his first marriage arranged for him by a senior male member of his own lineage, usually his mother's brother or *malalap* (big man). The *malalap* will often ask his sister's son or *fatui* (eyebrow) if he has a certain girl in mind as a potential wife, but just as often the arrangements will ignore any such preference; open dislike between the two, though, would prohibit any such marriage. Marriages other than those arranged by a real or classificatory *malalap* can be arranged by any senior man of the potential husband's lineage. Several years ago an elder classificatory brother of a Mòngalïfach (M-II) man arranged a marriage for his *bwïs* (brother) with a Sauwel (Leihao) girl. The young man's *malalap* was not on Lamotrek at the time, but staying on Lamaliur while making a canoe. When he returned he found that his *fatui* had been married for two months. The *malalap* did not approve of this marriage (some say because he himself had wished to marry the girl but had been refused); thus he went to the girl's mother and complained of the match, then told his *fatui* he must leave the girl, which the latter did. The *malalap* can not only arrange the first marriage of a man but he can also prohibit any such marriage he does not approve, for he is not looked upon as just an elder but as the representative of the lineage or descent group for that individual. Marriages subsequent to the first are left to the discretion of the individuals involved. They are not arranged and are usually not disrupted by the lineages concerned unless a question of incest arises. A man who takes a second wife, after having divorced the first, will usually be of such maturity as to recognize the best interests of his lineage and he will not contract a marriage which might be unwise. A Mòngalïfach informant held that in pre-contact times there were restrictions on interclan marriage that do not now exist. He held that individuals of chiefly clans could only marry individuals from one of the other chiefly clans. With the exception of intra-Mòngalïfach marriage (discussed below) there seems to be no tendency toward this or any other pattern of restricted marriage between clans today.

A marriage is characterized by a minimum of ceremony. Usually the man will move to the *bwogat* of the woman and on the following day the man's lineage will send a gift of cooked breadfruit or taro to the woman's lineage. One or two days later the woman's lineage will reciprocate with a similar gift to the husband's lineage. A slight variation on this pattern exists on Satawal, where the gift exchange involves goods other than food, i.e., cloth, *tur*, etc. In a second or subsequent marriage even this minimal gift exchange may not take place.

Divorce is most often initiated by the husband and it is easily obtained. A man may decide to leave his wife for one or several reasons ranging from economic to sexual differences. One informant stated that he divorced his first wife because the members of her *bwogat* were making him spend too much time working for it so that he did not have enough time to devote to his own lineage (patterns of labor are discussed in Chapter 4). Because of matrilocality it is simpler for a man to initiate a divorce than it is for a woman. A man would merely have to return to his own homestead whereas a woman would either have to force the man to leave or herself move to another. Because the latter is difficult, in those instances where a woman wishes to leave her husband she (and her lineage) will usually make his life so uncomfortable at their *bwogat* that the husband will eventually return to his own homestead of his own accord. There is no payment or gift return made to formalize a divorce unless a question of wife stealing is involved. Wife stealing or gross infidelity usually takes one of two forms. In the first a wife will desert her husband for another man.

For example, during the years of Japanese administration many men were taken from the island to work on Palau and Yap. One of these men, when he returned, found that his first wife had married another man in his absence. The woman's lineage was obligated to give the lineage of her first husband 20 *tur* and two axes before the latter felt that proper restitution had been made. Gross infidelity on the part of a wife has similar results. A man of Sauwel returned to his wife's house one night to find a Mongalïfach man with her. As is customary on such occasions, the husband went through the village on the way to his own lineage *bwogat* raising a cry against this insult while the Mongalïfach man rapidly made for his own homestead. Shortly thereafter, the husband arrived with his Sauwel lineage mates at the Mongalïfach *bwogat*, where they proceeded to go through the dwelling and canoe houses taking all material items that they desired. The Mongalïfach residents could offer no resistence, although in the past it is said that chiefly clans had some protection against such retribution taken by a nonchiefly clan. In those days any item which they wished to keep they could place overhead in the rafters of the dwelling house, where nonchiefly individuals were not allowed to search, as areas above one's head are generally taboo. In this particular case, though, no such restriction was observed, so Sauwel made off with numerous items ranging from pots, skirts, twine, and knives to larger objects like two paddling canoes and one sailing canoe. The lineage of the erring wife was also sacked by the Sauwel people that same night. My informant, who was the Mongalïfach man involved, said that no action was taken against him by his own lineage and he was told by his lineage head or *malübwogat* (man of the homestead) that if he so desired he could bring the wife to his own homestead to live, which my informant eventually did, but only after three days. For three days after the affair the Mongalïfach paramour hid on the ocean side of the island in order to avoid the laughter and ridicule of other villagers, only returning to his own homestead at night in order to eat and sleep. My informant said it was not customary for one's own lineage to penalize such behavior for it is recurrent with each generation. In fact, he said, he remembered when the present *malübwogat* had been involved in a similar affair when he was a youth. At that time the offended husband's lineage had come to the *bwogat* and even stripped the wall boards from the houses. If a paramour is not the cause of a divorce a wife may leave her husband without making a divorce payment just as he may leave her, but in this case she will have to leave her own *bwogat* if she is living matrilocally. She can return to this *bwogat* after the husband has returned to his.

The question of exogamy is one of the most involved on Lamotrek, and one which reflects the changing conditions under which this society operates and to which it must adapt. Informants in all clans but one insisted that marriage between clan mates was not permitted. Mòngalïfach was the only clan which did not insist on this restriction and in which intra*hailang* marriages were recorded. Figure 2 demonstrates that Mòngalïfach intramarriage has been occurring for at least five generations. It proved difficult to make inquiries about this type of marriage: many Mòngalïfach members were sensitive to such questions. On one occasion the clan affiliation of a woman involved in an intraclan marriage was concealed from me, and another ·time several Lamotrek men were particularly sensitive to a critical remark made by a Trukese visitor concerning this type of marriage. One attempt to justify intraclan marriage was made by an informant who said there were "two different Mòngalïfach *hailang*." Historically this is highly doubtful not only because of the unity of name, but also because Mòngalïfach is a clan widespread throughout the atolls of the Western Carolines and, as far as this writer knows, this is the only island where such an assertion is made. These informants were probably emphasizing the distinction between subclans which are developing into separate clans (see pp. 51-54). Area of residence and subclan size in relation to the size of the total population of the island are certainly two factors of importance in such clan fission.

The four subclans of Mòngalïfach are formed of six lineages. These can be identified in Figure 2 as follows:

Subclans	Lineages and Their Heads
M-I: Lualimat	M-1: Lefaioup (*tamolùfalu*)
M-II: Liak	M-2: Umai
	M-3: Tagilimal
	(M-5: see M-IV below)
M-III: Liang	M-4: Yoromai
M-IV: Laisimiat	M-5: Igùfail
(now independent of M-II)	(descent line of Lùmetabusho, nearly an independent M-6)

At one time the members of M-IV resided in the northern district of Lamotrek and were merely a component lineage of M-II subclan. Tagilimal states that in those times the lineage of Igùfail had rights to the political chieftainship and property of M-II just as M-2 and M-3 now do, and, in addition, none of these three lineages could intermarry. However, when Igùfail changed the seat of his lineage from the north to Onesh in the south and thus came under the jurisdiction of Hatamang, its membership in M-II was lost along with the rights of that subclan. M-5 then became an independent subclan in its own right and intermarriage with the other subclans of the clan was permitted. As Figure 2 shows, there is no recorded instance of intraclan marriage within the subclan boundaries; and subclan boundaries correspond to the three district divisions. Before the migration of M-IV the number of districts equaled the number of subclans of this clan. Within Mòngalìfach, then, the rule of subclan exogamy is the counterpart of clan exogamy among the other *hailang* of the island. This would seem to indicate a complete fission taking place within Mòngalìfach.

The five completely independent lineages of Mòngalìfach are resident on the following homesteads: M-1, the lineage of the paramount chief, is from Fairochekh in the southern district; M-2 is localized in the north at Hapilamahal; M-3 adjoins the holdings of M-2 and is centered at Olipùpù; M-4 has Hapalam as its lineage seat and it is held that traditionally this is the Mòngalìfach lineage of lowest status, for the members of it are said to have migrated here long after the other lineages were established on the island; the genealogical evidence of Figure 2 indicates, though, that the lineage has been on the island at least six generations. An explanation of the ranking of M-IV (M-5) will require a discussion of Hatamang clan and the functions of adoption in Western Carolinian society.

Hatamang clan in 1962-63 had a total membership of only seven, yet its land holdings and political position are such as to necessitate greater numbers for both exploitation and administration. The functions of Saur *hailang* in the political and economic organization of the island were even more seriously jeopardized when that clan became extinct; it was solved, though, when patrilaterally related individuals resident on Saur land assumed the functions of true Saur members. In the case of Hatamang, adoption has provided a means of continuity without alteration of political organization.

An adopted child on Lamotrek assumes nearly all the rights and obligations of a natural child toward his adoptive parents while retaining those descent and inheritance privileges due his true lineal position. The adoption of a child is always arranged before its birth. The couple who wish to adopt the child will approach the pregnant woman and her husband and ask for their approval. This is either given or denied by the couple, possibly after consulting more senior members of their lineages before reaching a decision. On Lamotrek half of all the children in 1962-63 who were 16 years of age and below had been adopted. The percentage on Satawal was even higher: more than three-fourths of the children had adoptive parents. Since the transaction is arranged before birth there is little difference between the number of boys adopted and the number of girls. Fifty per cent of the Lamotrek adoptions were contracted either matrilaterally or patrilaterally. That is, a woman will adopt a child of the same clan affiliation (but usually of different lineage or descent line) as herself; or a member of the father's clan or lineage will adopt one of his children. This practice, then, serves to reinforce interlineage matrilateral or patrilateral kin ties, especially when the residence of the child is changed to the *bwogat* of the adoptive parents. A child does not usually move from his homestead of birth to that of his adoptive parents until he is four or five years of age and even after the move he might alternate residence between the two homesteads until marriage. The rights and obligations of an adoption may be recognized only for the life of the individual or may last into later generations, or the adoption can be nullified if both of the lineages involved so desire. In this last case ceremonial gift exchange, appropriate role and status behavior, and labor obligations between the adopted and adoptive individuals are ignored. If an adopted individual establishes residence at marriage on his true lineage land (as is the usual case with a woman) or on his wife's land (in the case of a man), then his adopted status will be considered more or less inactive. On the other hand, if postmarital residence is maintained on the land of his (or her) adoptive lineage then his rights to this land, as well as the rights of any children of this marriage, are reinforced. An adopted individual is restricted in marrying into the adoptive matriclan as well as into his true clan. That is, if residence is maintained after marriage on one's adoptive homestead, then one's children will be prohibited from marrying into the lineage of that homestead (but not necessarily its clan). There are three general occasions when residence is maintained on adoptive land: (1) When one's true lineage has otherwise become extinct one will often remain on adoptive land in order to be with kinsmen who will help in the exploitation of resources and the necessary labor of everyday living. (2) One will often remain on adoptive land with one's descent line when all members of the adoptive group have died. In this way the adopted individual, by means of these ties, maintains control over the land. (3) When one has been adopted by a lineage residing on another island and while resident there marries, one will often be reluctant to return to the island of birth.

The present political position of lineage M-5 can be traced to the second condition stated above. This lineage can trace a close relationship to a now extinct Mòngalïfach lineage of Falihoal *bwogat*. M-5, however, is centered at Onesh, and the senior man of this lineage, who is naturally Mòngalïfach, is the chief of Hatamang clan. Igùfail is this person and he continues to claim Falihoal as land of his lineage. Nevertheless, he is unable to exercise any real jurisdiction over it since no member of his lineage has maintained residence upon it. Falihoal is also claimed by members of lineage M-4, and they are able to build a stronger case for their control because of the proximity of Falihoal to Hapalam, the seat of this lineage.

Igùfail and his lineage are able to justify their claim to the chieftainship of Hatamang in the following way. Four or more generations ago a female member of M-5 was adopted by the Hatamang residents of Onesh (and at that time Bwolipi) *bwogat*. This lineage of Hatamang died out but the descendants of the adopted Mòngalïfach woman continued to reside at this homestead. Today, only one other lineage of Hatamang remains on the island centered at Iaopïl. This lineage and its homestead were inferior in status to that which inhabited Onesh-Bwolipi. The land holdings of Hatamang clan are extensive, though, and in order for M-5 to retain control of its share of these holdings it became centered at Onesh and, sometime later, a descent line settled Peiliwer. Today, then, the Hatamang chieftainship is associated not only with true Hatamang but also with M-5, the residents of Onesh. The political and economic privileges are shared by both and when the most senior male member of the two lineages, as is the case now, comes from

Plate 10. Igûfail, chief of the southern district and of Hatamang clan, with his wife, her daughter, and their two young adopted children.

M-5 he is justified in claiming the chieftainship due Hatamang clan; this claim is disputed neither by true Hatamang members nor by other clans and lineages of the island. Established residence and control of the land parcels involved via adoption are justification enough for the claim to be legitimate. The case might be different and the claim certainly less definite if the members of M-5 did not live on Hatamang land.

This absorption of M-5 into the polity of Hatamang has also resulted in an adjustment within Mòngalïfach clan to which M-5 legitimately belongs. Intermarriage now occurs between M-5 and the other Mòngalïfach lineages; thus it has achieved the status of an independent subclan and classification here as M-IV. Genealogical evidence indicates that M-5 was marrying into M-3 as many as five generations ago, hence the adoption of M-5 by Hatamang must have taken place two or more generations before this. One informant, when questioned on this topic, stated that at one time intermarriage was not allowed between M-5 and M-2 or M-3, "but since they [M-5] moved to the other end of the island we are no longer closely related." This complex of circumstances—the fact that the homesteads of these lineages are distant and in different island districts, the close association which exists between a homestead and a lineage, and the assumption of the duties, rights, and obligations, not only of a different lineage, but also of a different clan, by the adopted one—all contribute to the present state of affairs. Territoriality, or the equating of critical spatial distance (see discussion of districts below) with kin distance has encouraged intermarriage between M-4 and other Mòngalïfach lineages, too. M-4 not only arrived on Lamotrek much later than the other lineages of this clan, but it also came from Woleai—an island some distance from Lamotrek. An additional factor which contributes to the acceptance of intraclan marriage, though, must be the size of Mòngalïfach with respect to the total population of the island. The limited number of potential spouses available to any Mòngalïfach individual, especially when additional fictive kin ties established by adoption are taken into account, has probably encouraged intraclan marriage as a means to widen the field of potential mates.

THE DISTRICT

The delineation of political groups and the authority of chiefs has a basis in locality as well as kin group affiliation, as suggested above in the discussion of both *bwogat* and localization of subclan land holdings. The interrelationship of the factors of locality, kinship, and political status is most clearly reflected in the *tabw* (district).

Lamotrek Island, and particularly the settlement area, is divided into three districts—Ifang (North), Lugulapùlïfalu (Large Center of the Island) which is usually simply called Lugulap (Large Center), and Iur (South). The approximate boundary lines of these districts are noted on Map 9. When this map is compared to Maps 6, 7, and 8 the district boundaries closely approximate the main land-holding areas of the three chiefly clans: Mòngalïfach (north), Saufalacheg (middle), and Hatamang (south). Mòngalïfach, the

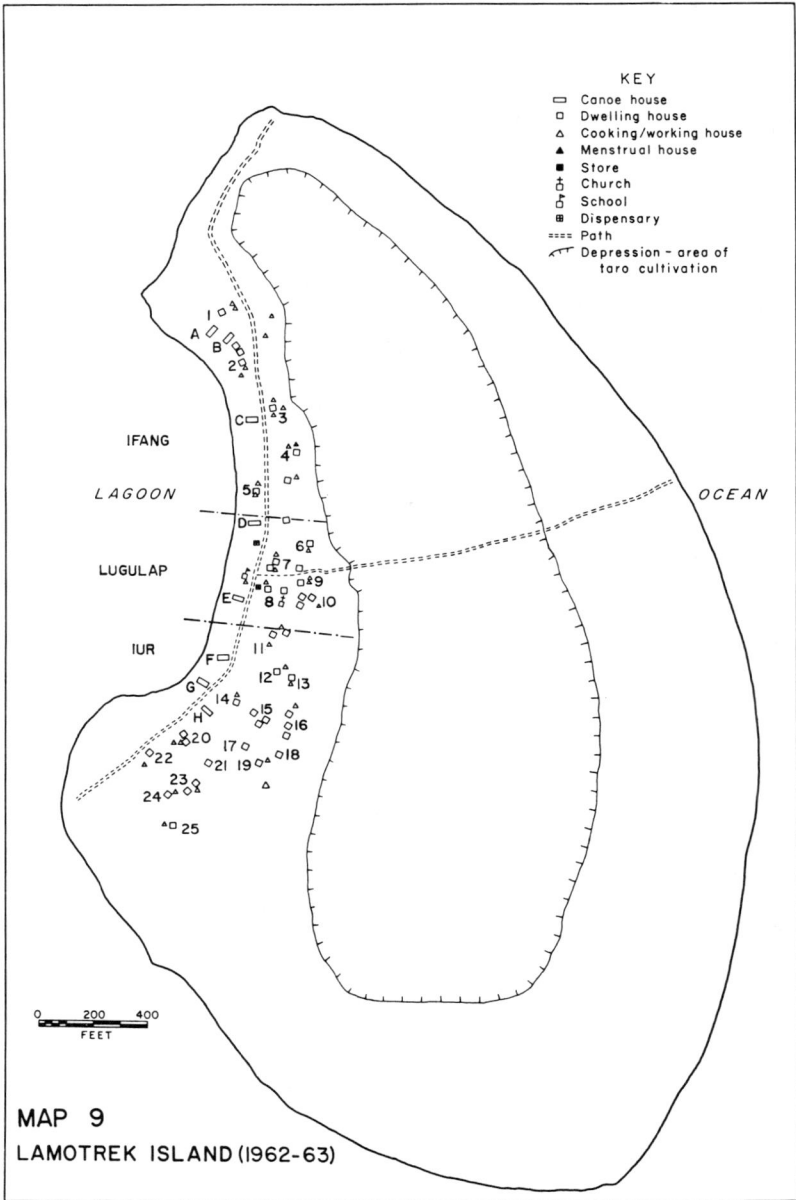

KEY
□ Canoe house
□ Dwelling house
△ Cooking/working house
▲ Menstrual house
■ Store
⊕ Church
⊟ School
⊞ Dispensary
==== Path
Depression – area of
     taro cultivation

IFANG

LAGOON

LUGULAP

IUR

OCEAN

0 200 400
FEET

MAP 9
LAMOTREK ISLAND (1962-63)

clan of the paramount chief, is the only chiefly clan which controls considerable blocks of land in all three districts. The lagoon
and reef of the atoll are owned exclusively by the three chiefly
hailang with the holdings of Mongalïfach subdivided among its
lineages (Map 10). Although the paramount chief comes from
Fairochekh *bwogat* the most important piece of land on the island
is not this homestead but Lamïtakh, which lies between Kulong
and Lugal canoe houses and is bounded on the east by the path
and the west by the lagoon. Lamïtakh is the land on which the
men's house once stood (and where its ruins can still be seen)
and the plot which symbolizes the authority of the *tamolüfalu*.
When the paramount chief issues a directive it is often paraphrased
as being "word from Lamïtakh." Oddly, though, Lamïtakh belongs
to Sauwel and not to Mongalïfach. It is possible, although I have
no evidence to prove it, that Lamïtakh may once have belonged
to Mongalïfach but was transferred to Sauwel, as were numerous
other parcels, when M-I began to near extinction. In either case,
though, Sauwel may own and exploit the land agriculturally, but
neither they nor anyone else may build a structure on this land
without the permission of the *tamolüfalu*; and there is no evidence
that any such building has stood on this land since the men's house
(*fal-lap*) was abandoned around 1860. The authority of the paramount chief, then, is felt and symbolized in all districts of the island and, as will be shown later, between islands. In addition each
of the three districts is represented by a *tamolnïtabw* (chief of the
district) who is drawn from the chiefly clan which predominates
in that district. Thus, although there are only three chiefly clans
and three districts there are four *tamol*—one *tamolüfalu* and three
tamolnïtabw. Mongalifach *hailang*, then, has two chiefs drawn from
its ranks, for the *tamolüfalu* cannot act as the northern district
chief, since this position is attached to a southern district *bwogat*.
Under normal circumstances there would be no confusion about
the authority of each district chief. Today, though, because of the
limited ability of the *tamolüfalu* and the fact that she has delegated
some of her duties to the Ifang district *tamolnïtabw*, confusion does
occur. On the one hand, individuals may sometimes complain about
the decisions of the Ifang *tamol* and justify their complaints on the
basis that he is not the *tamolüfalu*, thus ignoring the fact that
the paramount chief has appointed him to act as such. And on the
other hand, the Ifang *tamol* is often reluctant either to reach or

press his decision on supradistrict affairs, for even though he has accepted the appointment as acting paramount chief, he is well aware of his true status position. For both of these reasons, then, the Ifang *tamol* will usually delay reaching a decision until he has not only consulted wih the true *tamolúfalu* but also with the other district chiefs and the senior man of M-2, who is a rival for power within M-II. Several informants criticized this course of action because it resulted in delayed decisions or no decisions at all; the position of acting paramount chief in a society with a clearly defined status hierarchy is difficult, to say the least.

The present *tamol* of Lamotrek and the domains over which they preside are as follows:

Tamolúfalu	Tamollïhailang	Tamolnïtabw
Lefaioup	Lefaioup (Móngalïfach)	Tagilimal (Ifang)
	Ligiol (Saufalacheg)	Ligiol (Lugulap)
	Igúfail (Hatamang)	Igúfail (Iur)

Each of these chieftainships is associated with the following locality:

Tamolúfalu	Tamollïhailang	Tamolnïtabw
Lamïtakh	Móngalïfach-Fairochekh	Ifang-Hapilamahal
(today Lugal)		(or Falihoal)
	Saufalacheg-Faligiliau	Lugulap-Faligiliau
	Hatamang–Onesh-Bwolipi	Iur–Onesh-Bwolipi

The status differential between ordinary *bwogat* and homesteads of chiefs is recognized by a terminological difference. The *bwogat* of a chief is properly referred to not by this term, but as an *erao*. There are five homesteads which are presently called *erao* on Lamotrek—Fairochekh, Falihoal, Hapilamahal, Faligiliau, and Bwolipi (Onesh). When these *erao* are compared with the actual *bwogat* of origin of the present chiefs of the island two discrepancies are noted. First, the chief of the northern district is a man of Olipúpú—not Hapilamahal or Falihoal. Here seems to be the basis of the dispute between the senior men of M-2 and M-3 concerning their relative status, which came into the open when Lefaioup appointed an acting paramount chief. Second, the chief of Saufalacheg is a man of Chiligilafa, not Faligiliau. The relative status of the two lineages involved here was discussed earlier. The evidence seems to indicate, then, that an *erao* is *the homestead of the senior lineage with rights to the chieftainship*. In any par-

Plate 11. Repairs under way at Urieitakh canoe house.

ticular generation, depending on the availability of men, the actual chief may be drawn from one of the other lineages of the subclan, but inheritance rights fall first to the lineage of the *erao*. If this explanation is valid then Falihoal is probably of higher status than Hapilamahal. The latter has most likely only been considered an *erao* since the extinction of the lineage of Falihoal. Igúfail and his lineage could probably have pressed a claim to this *erao* if they had not moved to Onesh-Bwolipi.

Whereas the authority of a *tamollihailang* extends to all members of his clan and non-members using facilities belonging to his clan (e.g., affines living uxorilocally on a clan *bwogat* or using a clan canoe house; non-kin who have received gifts from the clan and are obliged to provide periodic *paliwen*, etc.), the authority of a *tamolnïtabw* extends to all individuals who are residing in the district regardless of their clan affiliation. It is on the basis of this latter authority that chiefly clans direct the activities of nonchiefly clans. And similarly, it is this concept of territoriality that allows the *tamolüfalu* to direct the activities of all island residents regardless of clan affiliation. Even though the rights of a chief derived from the multiple sources of kinship and territoriality, the decision of one chief would not often come into conflict with that of another. The authority of a chief does not include the right to adjudicate disputes. Land ownership disputes, for example, are the concern of the kin groups involved. A chief is consulted about such a dispute only when his kin group is a party to it—and in this case his chiefly status does not necessarily mean that a settlement will be in his favor. In this instance the chief could only direct activities if the dispute broke into open argument or conflict. He is, then, responsible for keeping the peace, and he would direct his clan members or district residents to cease fighting and settle the dispute peaceably. The keeping of the peace and decision-making with regard to unexpected events are occasions when the chiefs impose their judgments on island residents with little or no forewarning. The other occasions when a chief decides on a course of action are usually expected and repetitive. In these instances the extent of the chief's decision will only involve initiating and directing activities; participants will know what their own response should be because the events are expected and repetitious. An example from each of the chiefs' spheres of influence should clarify this.

The people of Lamotrek recognize that each visit of the trading ship (at intervals of three months) results in an outbreak of sickness on the island—usually the common cold. Before the predicted arrival of the vessel, then, the *tamolüfalu* directs all the inhabitants of the island to make and consume a prophylactic medicine which it is hoped will limit the seriousness of the *tümailitat* (sickness of the sea). The senior *waliyalus* (vehicle of the spirits, i.e., medium) will usually direct the preparation of the medicine, and when it is ready all residents of the island will gather, either at Lamïtakh or some other central location, to consume it. All residents know what their particular role is on such an occasion, but it is necessary for the *tamolüfalu* to initiate the activity before it is carried out. The paramount chief has a similar function in other island-wide concerns, e.g., dance contests, regulation of drinking, control of public property and disposal of public funds, island-wide religious and economic functions, etc.

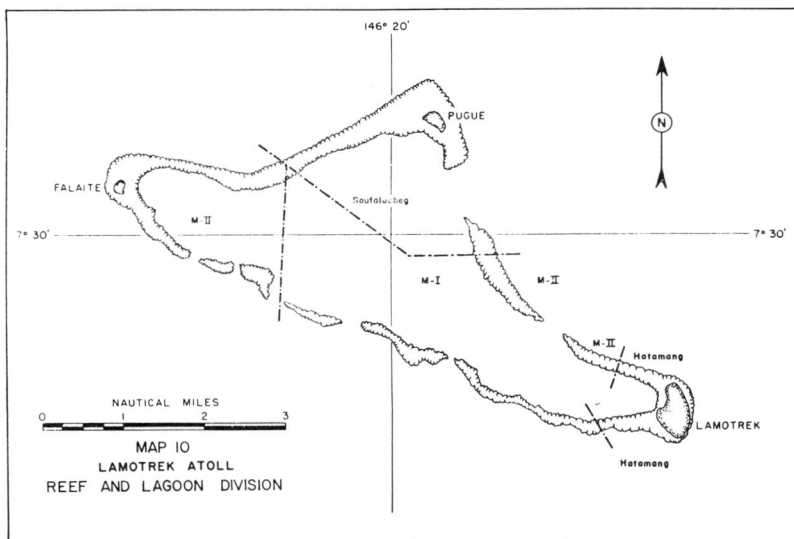

MAP 10
LAMOTREK ATOLL
REEF AND LAGOON DIVISION

The authority of the *tamollïhailang* is exercised within a more limited group and only when his clan is directly concerned. There are certain rights and ceremonies which are limited to chiefly clan members on Lamotrek. One of these is the *shalif* ceremony. When a woman of one of the chiefly *hailang* has her first pregnancy, her clan and that of her husband carry out a *shalif* in her honor before the birth of the child. It is the duty of the *tamollïhailang* to initiate and supervise this ceremony, which involves dancing at the canoe houses of the woman and her husband and the exchange of gifts. A woman of a nonchiefly clan is not entitled to a *shalif*. A *tamollïhailang* also has the right to make the reef and lagoon, as well as some of the land, of his clan *etabw* (taboo) after the death of a clan member. In the case of the reef and lagoon, where all island residents usually have the right to fish, this will prevent them, as well as the actual clan members of the chiefly *hailang*, from exploitation of the area for the duration of the *etabw*.

The *tamolnïtabw*, who is often also a *tamollïhailang*, has authority which extends beyond the boundaries of his own kin group to all residents of the district. The ceremony where this is most apparent is the *malïmei*, the first fruits ceremony of the breadfruit harvest. *Malïmei* ceremonies are carried out in June or July, when the breadfruit trees begin to bear in quantity. Informants said the ceremony on Lamotrek differed from the *malùmei* of Woleai and Ulithi, where the whole community contributed to the gathering and redistribution of the fruit. On Lamotrek each of the districts performs the ceremony separately. Fruit for consumption can be taken from a tree as soon as it begins to bear, but it is not until the breadfruit is available in quantity that the district chief schedules the annual *malùmei*. The chief, as head of the district and clan, informs clan mates and district residents via his *tela* and *ochang* of the date for the ceremony. All clan members and district residents of nonchiefly clans are expected to contribute labor and fruit from their tree holdings. District residents of chiefly clans other than the one organizing the *malùmei* are only required to contribute labor to the ceremony since they will be contributing fruit to the comparable ceremony of their own chiefly clan when it is carried out in one of the other districts. Breadfruit trees, as well as coconut palms, are often presented as gifts by individuals or kin groups to representatives of other kin groups on occasions similar to those previously discussed in the exchange of land. Recipients of such tree gifts not only provide *paliwen* to donors on the appropriate occasions, but also they must provide fruit from those trees for the *malùmei* ceremony of the donor clan, if the trees are located in the district of that chiefly clan. The uncooked breadfruit is assembled at the canoe house of the district chief—Ifang, either Urieitakh or Leibwul; Lugulap, Kulong; Iur, Yapùi—and there it is redistributed to the whole village.

Each district might carry out this ceremony on the same day or on different days; redistribution involves the total population, but assembling is restricted to district residents and the appropriate chiefly clan mates.

In the examples cited above a *tamol* will usually respond in a patterned way. Day-to-day and year-to-year living on Lamotrek, or any similar island, is consistent enough so that most decision-making situations have been met before in the lives of the individuals involved. A particular course of action, depending on the relevant circumstances, is recognized as the proper course of action by the chiefs and most of the inhabitants. The measure of a "good" or "bad" chief, then, is not in his ability to provide novel or unusual solutions to old problems, but rather in his ability to initiate and supervise at the proper time those responses which are well known among the inhabitants. The "bad" chief is the individual who delays such action or who hedges in decision-making.

Interdistrict activities, such as clearing public paths or repairing public buildings, which require laborers from all clans, are organized somewhat differently. The task may be initiated by the paramount chief or by the three district chiefs after consultation. The laborers are organized on the basis of district affiliation but those from Lugulap are invariably consolidated with those from Ifang and Iur. The triadic district organization thus becomes dualistic. On the specified day the workers will assemble in the two groups. Leomar *bwogat* is usually considered to be on the line which divides the two districts, and the residents of this homestead thus have the choice of working with either district. Men who are living uxorilocally will usually join the group representing their district of residence rather than that of origin, if these differ. When the work requires several days to complete the two groups often contribute labor on alternate days. In this way the men of both areas are able to continue day-to-day activities with as little prolonged disruption as possible. The cleaning and repairing of paths is a job which involves female as well as male workers; a sexual division of labor, therefore, cuts across the usual district division. The women form one labor group and the men another regardless of district of residence, but the island is still divided into two work districts and each sex is assigned to work in one. The women will work under the supervision of the senior female members of the chiefly clans as the males are supervised by the chiefs. Path cleaning is done twice a year and the district to which each sex is assigned is alternated every six months.

It is possible, of course, that dualism for the purposes of communal labor is merely another reflection of the effects of depopulation. Today, with fewer inhabitants on the island, it may no longer be profitable to attempt to maintain triadic labor groups. This does not seem likely, though, when one notes the numerous other manifestations of dualism in Lamotrekan organization and thought. Dualistic concepts also prevail in divination (*bwei*). One method depends on the number of knots which are tied into two pairs of coconut frond leaves and counted in units of four for an omen, while another method interprets the pattern formed by coconut oil on each side of the surface of a container of medicine. The container is divided by an imaginary line and the pattern on the right will predict whether many men will become sick while the pattern on the left will do likewise for the women. Dualism is symbolized further in the words for "left" and "right": left can be *peigùshabwut* (woman's side) or *peigengao* (bad side), while right is *peigùmal* (man's side) or *peigïhatch* (good side). Medicine is prepared from ingredients which are added in two's or multiples of two; and it is consumed either twice a day or over a period of two days. Numerous other dualistic concepts could be cited and some will be mentioned later in economics (marine *vs.* agricultural, interior *vs.* beach, canoe house *vs.* dwelling house) and in religion ("good" ghosts *vs.* "bad," spirits of the sky *vs.* spirits of the sea).

As Lévi-Strauss (1963:132-163) has suggested, dualistic and triadic concepts are not necessarily contradictory; one may imply or depend on the other. The settlement pattern of Lamotrek is certainly not in the form of a concentric village, but the triadic and dualistic forms noted above suggest this form rather than a diametric one (simple dualistic opposition). The hierarchy of clans does not conflict with this conceptualization. It was suggested earlier that Saufalacheg did not control land holdings which accurately reflected its status as second-ranking clan. As the "center" of an opposition between north and south, it would not need to. Folklore on Lamotrek mentions that in the past a sharper distinction was made between north and south on the island. Informants said that in those days it was dangerous for a northern man to walk in the southern district after nightfall for he might be attacked. And on this island, less than a mile long, there used to be a recognized linguistic difference between the north and south. Today this dialectal difference is only retained in a few words, but it is still recognized, as the people of the north say *bwutokh* (come here) and laugh at the people of the south who say *bwitokh*. Northern district residents also claim that the women of that district weave better *tur* and make better garlands than those of the south. In all of these discussions no mention is made of Lugulap and its people. Lugulap and Saufalacheg probably retain their position as mediatory between north and south. The function of the Saufalacheg chief as the mediator between the people of Lamotrek and the foreign administrators would certainly support this. I shall discuss this in greater detail in a later chapter. In pre-contact times, when marriage of a chiefly clan member was restricted to being with an individual from another chiefly clan, exchange of personnel would usually occur between districts. Although the restriction no longer applies, it is true that district exchange retains an importance which is reflected in intra-Mòngalïfach marriage, based on the triadic division of the island. Although admittedly theoretical, it is possible that Mòngalïfach symbolizes the unity of the island and its dualistic/triadic features. Mòngalïfach is dominant in the north—which in many ways is viewed as the most prestigious district of the island—but it is also predominant in the south, for this is the district of the paramount chief and the *bwogat* seat of subclan M-I. Pragmatically, Mòngalïfach provides the political and residential unity for the island which the role of paramount chief symbolizes.

SUMMARY

The kinship and political organization of Lamotrek emphasizes a system of status-ranked· chiefly and nonchiefly matriclans which can be divided into component subclans, lineages, and descent lines, each with particular kinds of rights to land and titles. Territorial ties—district and homestead—are of equal importance in the regulation of political activities. Chiefly clan lands and districts were probably once more or less coextensive, but with alteration of land holdings and marriage rules the picture has changed within the last 200 years.

Western Carolinian atoll populations are very small; usually they do not exceed 500 individuals. Kinship and territorial distinctions subdivide this population into smaller component units which are liable to extinction through natural processes and disasters. A means of adjusting to the eventuality of loosing significant structural units is necessary if the system is to survive. Basically, this means that the matrilineal organization must be supplemented by alternative means of transferring land ownership and political titles from generation to generation. In this way new kin and territorial units can be formed to replace those which have become extinct. On Lamotrek these alternatives are based on patrilateral and adoptive kin ties combined with residence and exploitation of particular homesteads within specified districts. The triadic/dualistic characteristics of Carolinian organization are suited to readjustment and adaptable to change. The dualism of Lamotrek is not, in the terminology of Lévi-Strauss (1963:151), a static diametric form, but an example of the dynamic "concentric" type, which is often found associated with status-ranked kin groups.

4

Economic Activities

The economic potential of the environment and its actual exploitation will be of direct concern in this chapter. The environmental base common to Western Caroline atolls was outlined in Chapter 2. Production, distribution, and consumption of subsistence goods are all dependent on the kinship and territorial groups discussed in Chapter 3. Most agricultural work groups are made up of individuals resident on a *bwogat* and members of the lineage who have inheritance rights to this land, but who may be resident elsewhere because of the requirements of the matrilocal/uxorilocal rule of residence. Marine exploitation parties are usually formed of men who are associated with a particular canoe house rather than *bwogat*, since the former is the center of activity for a man.

The *bwogat* settlement pattern on Lamotrek is well adapted to the dispersed nature of the subsistence crops, as both agricultural and marine resources are most efficiently exploited by small teams of workers. The above circumstances often encourage the fragmentation or fission of kin groups, as when a descent line breaks away from its parent lineage in order to maintain control over recently acquired property. The social organization of Lamotrek is flexible enough to adjust to the changing forms and number of its component groups without altering its fundamental structure. Survival on the atoll does not demand that exploitation units be large or long-lived. Thus, an unexpected and rapid change in features of the resource

74

base of the island can be met with an equally rapid adjustment in the exploitation of it.

Some of the statistical information in this chapter may be more detailed than necessary, but I have included it both for comparative purposes and to give an idea of the economic efficiency of most exploitation activities.

LAND RESOURCES

Most of the vegetation found on Lamotrek, Elato, and Satawal is of some economic value to the inhabitants of these islands as a source of food, fiber, medicine, or construction material; much has multiple uses. Food crops fall into two major categories: roots/tubers and tree crops.

Root Crops

Cyrtosperma (bulókh) is by far the most plentiful and important root crop on the island. Nearly the whole of the interior swamp is devoted to its production. This taro swamp (*bwül*) covers 58 acres of the island, of which more than one-third is intensively cultivated. *Colocasia (uot)* is found interspersed in lesser amounts among the beds of *Cyrtosperma* in the more productive areas of the swamp (which are those regions farthest from the island's shoreline). The peripheral areas of the *bwül* not only have less *Colocasia*, but also are less intensively planted with *Cyrtosperma*. Here one finds numerous coconut palms and pandanus trees among the taro.

Several taro-plot counts were made. In areas of intensive cultivation *Cyrtosperma* and *Colocasia* averaged 36 plants per 100 square feet, or more than 15,000 plants to the acre. In the peripheral areas the *Cyrtosperma* density was less than half this figure: 15 per 100 square feet. Projecting these figures to the whole swamp means there are around 500,000 taro plants on the island, of which some 80 per cent are *Cyrtosperma*. These figures agree quite closely with those presented by Barrau for Melanesia (1958) and other areas of Micronesia (1961). Assuming an average yield per plant of one pound (in exceptional circumstances *Cyrtosperma* may grow at a rate as high as 1.6 pounds per year [Barrau 1961:43]) this would mean each acre has a potential output of 15,000 pounds. Barrau (1958:42) has suggested that 13,200 pounds per acre for

Plate 12. A woman and her daughter at Hapalam *bwogat* pounding taro in preparation for the day's meal.

irrigated *Colocasia*, a small plant, is a reasonable figure. In any case, under normal conditions, and considering the present population of Lamotrek, such a yield would provide an ample surplus of taro, which can be left in the ground to continue growing.

My figures, although not as complete as I would like, suggest that an average of 1.5 pounds of taro are consumed per person, excluding babies, on those days when taro is eaten. Breadfruit and other root and tree crops make up at least one-fourth of the agricultural food consumed, so that in an average year less than 100,000 pounds, or about one-fifth the available amount, of taro is eaten on the island. If, after a typhoon, breadfruit production were destroyed and some areas of the taro swamp inundated, consumption would have to exceed one-third the potential before there would be a danger that the agricultural area could not support the present population.[1] Furthermore, the shortage would have to exist for at least three years. Three to four years seems to be about the length of time it takes an atoll to recover from a severe typhoon. Thus, there is a distinct possibility that such a shortage could occur even though, under normal circumstances, Lamotrek could support a

[1] Jacques Barrau (1961:43) states, "*Cyrtosperma* tubers cannot be profitably harvested until they are at least three years old."

population two or three times as large as now inhabits the island without any increase in subsistence production. If the need ever arose, additional clearing and preparation could considerably boost production in the peripheral areas of the swamp.

Alocasia (*fille*), dry-land or elephant-ear taro, is not grown in the swamp and is not generally preferred as a food crop. This aroid may be found planted in scattered areas on the island, often close to a dwelling or canoe house. *Xanthosoma*, sweet potatoes, and arrowroot are cultivated but are of little importance.

Tree Crops

The two important tree crops are coconuts (*lü*) and breadfruit (*mai*). The first is nonseasonal and a mature tree will bear between 100 and 300 nuts a year (Emory 1944:30; Woodrow 1910:572). Breadfruit, on the other hand, is a seasonal producer and output is variable, depending on the age of the tree.

Whereas root crops usually only suffer storm damage when their growing area is inundated by salt water, tree crops are often damaged by winds of even small tropical storms. The density pattern of coconut and breadfruit trees reflects this fact (Table V). In 1962, four years after the highly destructive typhoon of 1958, yields from coconut trees were just returning to normal; breadfruit production was still below pre-typhoon output, but beginning to produce a small surplus. Surplus coconuts are sold as copra to the trading ship, and February of 1962 saw the first such post-typhoon sales.

The main breadfruit season begins in late May and continues until September; a few trees will bear fruit during December and January. In the past some breadfruit trees were found closer to the edges of the island, but these were the first to be destroyed by the high winds of the 1958 storm. A few of these are still standing, but they do not constitute a significant proportion of the crop. No breakdown was made between those breadfruit trees which were producing and those which were immature; however, the majority of them were immature and nonproducing. Surplus breadfruit is preserved in earth-pits commonly found in many areas of the Pacific. Preserved breadfruit is called *mar*.

The over-all less dense planting and exploitation of the ocean side of the island (as noted in Table V) may be attributed to poorer soil, prevailing winds, and the smaller return for the greater amount of labor involved in cultivating this area intensively. Informants

TABLE V. Tree Density[a]

Location	Tree Type	Density per Acre
In the vicinity of settlement	Mature coconut	122
	Immature coconut	157
	Banana plants	122
South end of the island, near the lagoon	Mature coconut	157
	Immature coconut	70
Lagoon side of the island, near the taro swamp	Mature coconut	70
	Immature coconut	157
	Banana plants	225
	Breadfruit	17
Ocean side of the island	Mature coconut	52
	Immature coconut	70
	Pandanus	52

[a] This table not only notes the agricultural potential of tree crops on Lamotrek, but it also reflects two other important factors: (1) The tree-crop zones of the island are suggested by the relative density of coconut palms near the settlement and on the lagoon side of the island as contrasted to the density of other productive trees near the taro swamp. Soil fertility is the main reason for the existence of such zones, as it is for the less densely planted ocean side of the island. (2) The after-effects of the 1958 typhoon are still noticeable in the relative proportion of immature to mature coconut palms. New trees were planted after the storm and many of these have not yet matured; thus they outnumber producing trees in most areas of the island.

stated that it was only in recent years (possibly late German times) that coconut trees, in any numbers, were planted on the ocean side of the taro swamp. Undoubtedly this occurred only as their value as a cash crop increased. One may infer from this that the rest of the island is able to provide enough coconuts for food and fiber for a population at least as large as is now living on the island.

Banana plants (included here as a tree crop) are plentiful; at least four species are present on Lamotrek. Although they are certainly not as important in the diet as taro and breadfruit, they are as significant as sweet potatoes and more important than *Alocasia*. They are frequently eaten by children when ripe, and, while still green, cooked for general consumption. Pandanus is of no importance as a food crop except in times of acute food shortage.

All of the above trees supply fiber and building materials. The coconut palm has a wide variety of uses including cordage, thatch, and wood for house construction. The wood and sap of the breadfruit tree is of prime importance in building canoes and houses.

Plate 13. A young woman grating coconut at Leomar *bwogat*.

Banana plant fiber (which is taken from the trunk of the plant) is of major importance for weaving fiber. Nearly every other species of tree which reaches significant size is utilized in some type of construction, be it building, canoe, clothing, or fishing apparatus.

Plate 14. Young tobacco plants protected by rings of stones growing near a
dwelling house.

Tobacco

Tobacco (*tümaho*) is an important agricultural crop. The plant
was introduced in Spanish times and is consumed in cigarette form
by about 90 per cent of the adult population. It is grown in small
plots near the houses of all inhabited homesteads and such plots
may have as few as four or five plants or more than 50.

A great deal of time is expended on tobacco production, especially in mulching and fertilization. The crop, though, does not
seem to flourish on all coral islands. Lamotrek has a great deal
more than does either Satawal or Elato. Its scarcity on Elato is
probably due to lack of labor; on Satawal a soil difference may
explain the shortage.

Animal Life

Fauna of economic importance is much less numerous than the
plant species noted above. All of the animals of major importance
are domesticated species. Pigs (*silo*), chickens (*mälukh*), and dogs

(*holókh*) are all present and eaten. Cats (*hatu*) are raised but not eaten.

The average number of domestic animals per homestead on Lamotrek is three pigs, nine chickens, and two dogs—this includes animals of all ages. The meat of the above is consumed only on special occasions or when fish, the usual protein, is scarce for five or more days. Dogs are kept both as pets and as livestock; a dog which is recognized as someone's pet is not eaten unless there is a critical shortage of meat. Pigs are the only livestock regularly and conscientiously fed by their owners; a slop of coconut meat and water is provided. Pigs are not allowed to run loose, but are tied by a foreleg to a tree on the homestead land of their owner.

Coconut crabs and other land crabs have minor importance as subsistence food. Birds are infrequently eaten because they are difficult to catch. The majority of those caught are taken from their nests while still too young to fly. This is not often done on Lamotrek itself, but is a practice common to workers, hunters, and fishermen visiting the neighboring uninhabited islands where the majority of the birds nest. Bird feathers have an importance as material for fish lures.

SEA RESOURCES

Reef and Lagoon

The majority of the sea resources exploited by the people of Lamotrek come from either the reef or the lagoon. As would be expected, fish are by far the most important and are plentiful during most of the year. Few fish species found in the waters of Lamotrek are poisonous to eat, although many are known to be so in the Marianas to the north. The only fish rejected as food are those poisonous to touch, those too small and difficult to obtain, sharks, rays, eels, and porpoises (the last are occasionally eaten).

Purple slate-pencil sea urchins are actively gathered by women and children for consumption during certain seasons of the year when the daytime tides are especially low. Clams, lobsters, and octopus are also eaten, but are considered inferior to fish in quality.

Open Ocean

Blue-water fish are of secondary subsistence importance on Lamo-

Plate 15. Children shelling sea urchins.

trek even though they are highly prized. Those most frequently taken include bonito (*harangap*), tuna (*taho*) and wahoo (*ngal*). Open-sea fishing is of greater importance for survival on Satawal, since this island lacks a lagoon where sheltered fishing can be done. The fringing reef of Satawal is fished the same as the Lamotrek and Elato lagoon reefs, but its small size does not provide sufficient fish for the entire population. Thus, approximately 50 per cent of the fishing on Satawal is directed toward the open ocean around the island or on the reef and lagoon of Pikhailo (West Fayu).

Turtles

Turtles (*wóng*) are an important food source to the people of all three of these islands. The green sea turtle is plentiful during the months of April, May, and June, and is present in smaller numbers throughout the rest of the year. This species of turtle usually averages more than 200 pounds when caught; most of this weight is edible flesh and viscera.

The turtle is wary of coming near an inhabited region of an island and hence is most frequently taken on an uninhabited island or on the ocean side of an atoll island. They are usually caught when they come ashore at night to lay eggs. The people of Lamotrek frequently hunt turtles on Pugue, Falaite, and Olimarao. Less frequent trips are made to Lamaliur. The residents of Elato hunt turtles on Falipi and Lamaliur. Satawalese must rely on Pikhailo and the windward side of their own island for turtles.

PATTERNS OF EXPLOITATION

Division of Labor

Division of labor along sexual lines is an important feature of Lamotrek organization. Even though the division is clear-cut there is no gross environmental sphere from which one or the other sex is completely excluded. A man's most important subsistence task is fishing while a woman's is gardening. If the need arises, though, men will assist in the harvesting of taro and women may help in certain marine tasks, such as turtle hunting, when there is a scarcity of men. But cultivation and fishing are the two tasks which are

TABLE VI. Sexual Division of Labor

Men's Work	Women's Work
1. *Marine*: fishing, turtling, reef gathering in deep water, e.g., lobsters, clams, octopi	1. *Marine*: reef gathering at low tide, e.g., sea urchins
2. *Agricultural*: coconut palm cultivation, harvesting, tapping; breadfruit harvesting; tobacco harvesting	2. *Agricultural*: cultivation and harvesting of taro, sweet potatoes, squash, tobacco cultivation; other harvesting, i.e., mountain apples, etc.
3. *Husbandry*: slaughter of dogs, pigs, chickens	3. *Husbandry*: feeding of dogs, pigs, chickens
4. *Construction and maintenance*: canoes, houses, twine, rope, looms, agricultural and fishing equipment; cleaning paths	4. *Construction and maintenance*: weaving, fiber preparation, mats and thatch; garlands; cleaning paths
5. *Domestic*: caring for children	5. *Domestic*: caring for children; preparing food; gathering firewood, water; preparing salt; cleaning
6. *Commercial*: gathering coconuts; extracting and drying copra; sacking, transporting, selling copra; gathering seashells	6. *Commercial*: extracting and drying copra

most sharply restricted along sexual lines, and only under extreme survival conditions are such lines crossed. Table VI has itemized the major subsistence tasks according to sex. Although this table gives some idea of the range of jobs which confront a resident of Lamotrek, it does not gauge the relative importance of nor the time expended on each. This will be done when cycles of activity are discussed.

Labor Groups

The size of a work group will naturally depend on the task to be completed, and thus will range from a single individual to the whole community. Exploitation groups, like units of distribution and consumption, have their primary basis in the *bwogat* and hence are based on residence and kinship. Those resident on a *bwogat*, as stated above, are usually members of a single lineage, plus inmarrying males and minus those who marry out. Nevertheless, because of depopulation and demographic changes, including the emergence of new lineages as well as the extinction of others, some *bwogat* may include all representatives of a clan, subclan, lineage, or lineage segment on the island.

Since the homestead is intimately associated with agricultural land it is to be expected that agricultural exploitation groups are usually composed from among its residents. Thus, it is most common for female work groups to be made up of consanguineal relatives and adopted female children. Conversely, men, who usually change their residence at marriage, most often form their work groups from the individuals affiliated with a particular canoe house. A man will usually affiliate with the canoe house of his homestead of residence. In this way, when a man marries and changes residence he will ordinarily join the canoe house group of his wife's clan or lineage, or of the district in which his new residence is located. Sometimes the determination of such canoe house affiliation becomes fairly involved.

By way of example, Umai is the senior male of Hapilamahal *bwogat*. As such, he is one of the highest-ranking men on the island since he represents a senior lineage of Mòngalifach clan. Leibwul canoe house, which is on Hapilamahal land (Map 9:2, B), is his canoe house by virtue of his birth. Umai is living uxorilocally, at Onïsal. His wife is from Satawal and of Hofalu clan—a clan which has no traditional land on Lamotrek. Onïsal *bwogat* belongs

Plate 16. Emoyang weaving a fish net.

to Mòngalïfach, but to a lineage other than Umai's. His wife is living here patrilaterally; that is, her father was Mòngalïfach and of this land, but now there are no members of his lineage surviving to claim the *bwogat*. Today, Hapalam, primarily because of its proximity, claims ownership of Onïsal and of Falamara canoe house. Thus, by virtue of his marriage Umai has rights and obligations at Falamara. The situation becomes even more involved because of an adoption and a land dispute. Umai, as a youth, was adopted by Igùfail, the chief of Hatamang clan, but because Igùfail is actually of M-5 descent, as explained in Chapter 3, he also makes a claim to Falamara and Onïsal land. The land claim and the adoption allow Umai to participate in the activities of Yapùi canoe house, which is the center for Hatamang men. Yapùi is also used by the men of Sauwel, for the structure is built on Sauwel land. Hatamang received permission from Sauwel to place its canoe house here because none of its own land in the district has suitable access to the lagoon.

No matter how simple or complex the relationship traced, the fundamental rules followed for affiliation to a canoe house are: (1) A man retains rights to and obligations at the canoe house of his matrilineage. (2) At marriage, a man gains certain rights to the use and obligations for the maintenance of the canoe house of his wife's matrilineage. (3) A man may claim similar rights to a canoe house traced by more distant relationships (e.g., adoption, patrilateral), if he is unable or unwilling to make a claim to one by a more direct matrilineal relationship.

In summary, the work groups based on members of a canoe house, then, can be quite varied, ranging from consanguineal kin to affinal kin to unrelated friends and district co-residents.

Cycles of Activity

During an average day 88 per cent of the adult women will participate in one or all the tasks of cultivation, harvesting, food preparation, and weaving. The work records I kept, on representative days over a six-month period, show that from September through early May (the non-breadfruit season) a woman will work an average of 6.5 hours per day at the above jobs, divided in the following way: 2.3 hours in the taro swamp cultivating and harvesting; 2.8 hours preparing and cooking the day's food; 1.3 hours

Plate 17. A young girl cleaning banana fiber which will be used in weaving.

Plate 18. Faholit tapping a coconut palm for toddy and wine production.

weaving; 0.1 hour in miscellaneous tasks. The average work group will be made up of three women. These statistics are computed from the day's activities of all female laborers. The average amount of time spent by a participant in a specific job is somewhat different; 3.0 hours in the taro fields; 3.2 hours preparing and cooking food; and 2.5 hours weaving.

There is a seasonal variation in women's labor correlated with the breadfruit season (mid-May through August). In these months a daily mean of 0.2 hours is spent in the taro swamp; 3.0 hours are spent in harvesting and preparing breadfruit for consumption; and 1.8 hours at loom weaving. Considering the actual participants in each chore, a woman still will not go to the taro swamp for less than two hours' work; she will spend 3.3 hours harvesting and cooking food and 3.0 hours at a sitting weaving. Women are able to devote less labor to breadfruit cultivation and harvesting than they would to taro production primarily because of the labor men contribute to breadfruit harvesting. Thus, the women have more time to devote to weaving during this season.

A man's labor is both daily and seasonally less routine than a woman's. The one task a man will complete each day, save when he is on his deathbed, is the tapping of four coconut palms for their sap. Half of the daily yield is consumed as a sweet toddy by the women and children and half is allowed to ferment and is drunk as a wine by the man himself. The chiefs have restricted each man to four trees for sap production; the taps are renewed three times a day, which amounts to a total time expenditure of 1.5 hours. In addition to the above, the daily chores of a man may include one or more of the following activities.

Communal fishing expeditions occur about twice each month (less frequently during November and December, when westerly winds prevail). On any other day of the month, except Sunday, 22 per cent of the men will be fishing, singly or in groups of various sizes. Each man will spend some 5.2 hours at the task and return with 9 pounds of fish, or 1.75 pounds per man-hour. There are three main fishing techniques: trap, line, and spear. Most fishing will take place in the lagoon and on or around the lagoon reef. Table VII compares the amount of time spent in each major fishing technique and the resulting percentage of the total yield. All three major techniques are closely correlated in time expended and yield.

TABLE VII. Fishing Techniques

Method	Time	Yield	Time/Trip	Yield/Man-hour
	(per cent)	(per cent)		
Traps	43	43	6 hrs.	1.6 lbs.
Hook/line	25	27	4.5 hrs.	1.8 lbs.
Spear	25	24	5 hrs.	1.5 lbs.
Other	7	6		

Environmental factors and the availability of equipment (e.g., traps, hooks, etc.) are often decisive in determining the choice of fishing methods from day to day. Eighty per cent of all trap fishing is done by men working alone. During the remaining 20 per cent of time devoted to this fishing method an average group of four men works together. This variation in work group size can be explained in the following way. When working those traps at some distance from the island several men are needed to handle the sailing canoe necessary for travel to these areas. On the other hand, traps close to the island, where the majority of them are, can be easily reached by one man in a paddling canoe. Similarly, line fishing is nearly always carried out near the island by a lone man in a paddling canoe. Line fishing in distant regions of the lagoon, while often resulting in large catches, is unprofitable from the standpoint of equipment loss, due both to the coral bottom (because of the stronger ·currents) and to the sharks, which are more numerous in these areas. Skin diving and spear fishing is the third major fishing technique and is probably of recent origin,

Plate 19.   Men preparing to take a fish trap into the water.

since it depends on steel for spears, rubber tubing or bands for propulsion, and glass for diving goggles. Nevertheless, today 25 per cent of all fishing is done in this way. In opposition to line fishing, spear fishing is done in the more distant areas of the lagoon, along the reef. It probably can be viewed as a substitute technique for these areas, where the line method would not prove profitable because of the high equipment loss mentioned. Spear-fishing groups, which average 3.25 men, illustrate that an efficient sailing canoe group is usually necessary. The remaining fishing time is spent in a variety of ways—nets, torches, open ocean trolling. Blue-water fishing is enjoyed by the men, but it is not often practiced on Lamotrek because of the hazards involved, the unreliability of the wind, and the low yield for the amount of time expended. This is not the case on Satawal, as previously mentioned, where a large proportion of fishing time is spent in open ocean trolling and the corresponding yields are much higher.

The man-hours involved in turtle hunting are difficult to compute. There is only one small area on Lamotrek island itself where turtles come ashore. This sandy beach is on the ocean side of the island north of the cross-island path. Table VIII shows that 23 per cent of the turtles taken in 1962-63 were caught there. In these instances it is usual for a single man, or perhaps two, to spend several hours waiting for a turtle to come ashore. He may have to wait two or three nights before a catch is made. A further 28 per cent of the turtles are taken within the atoll: 15 per cent on Pugue and 13 per cent on Falaite. Thus, over half of the turtles caught by Lamotrekans are taken from their own atoll. Turtle hunting at either Pugue or Falaite consumes more time than on

TABLE VIII. Turtles Caught by Lamotrekans (1962-63)

Island of Origin	4	5	6	7	8	9	10	11	12	1	2	3
Lamotrek	1	5	2	3	1	2	2	1	—	2	2	—
Pugue	—	9	—	—	—	1	—	—	—	—	—	4
Falaite	2	7	1	—	—	1	—	—	—	1	—	—
Olimarao	—	—	6	2	—	—	4	—	—	—	1	—
Lamaliur	7	—	5	—	—	—	—	—	—	—	5	2
Falipi	2	7	—	—	—	—	—	2	1	—	—	—
Total	12	28	14	5	1	4	6	3	1	3	8	6

Lamotrek Island. A sailing canoe is needed to get to these islands, thus a group of three or more men will make the trip. Hunting on Lamaliur, Falipi, and Olimarao will often be combined with copra production, fishing, or some other minor economic activity. In these cases one cannot say that the total time away from Lamotrek was devoted to turtle hunting, although that may have been the major purpose of the voyage. Canoes to these latter islands may be away from Lamotrek for two weeks before any turtles are caught. Of the 73 voyages made to uninhabited islands in 1962-63, 35 were made to hunt turtles, 36 were primarily to make copra, and 2 were made for other reasons (Table IX). All of the copra-making voyages were carried out from September through October and January through February; thus they anticipated the presumed arrival date of the trading ship. Only one voyage was made in November both because of poor weather and because of the expected arrival of the trading ship, which none of the men wished to miss.

Copra production, which is the only important commercial activity on Lamotrek, is primarily a man's responsibility. This is much as one would expect, since care and cultivation of coconut palms are a man's duty. The copra labor which women furnish is restricted to helping the men remove the meat from the shells and watching over it while it is sun-dried. Sun-drying of copra is the only method practiced on Lamotrek and Elato—Satawal, though, has several drying kilns. The heaviest labor involved in copra making, then, is exclusively done by men and includes gathering the nuts, cutting them open, sacking the finished product, and transporting it to Lamotrek (if it has been produced on one of the other islands). If there is no need to transport copra from one island to another, one man can produce approximately 75 pounds per day, which is the yield of about 225 nuts. A man would rarely

TABLE IX. Voyages to Uninhabited Islands

Island	4	5	6	7	8	9	10	11	12	1	2	3
						Month						
Pugue	—	2	—	2	1	8	5	—	2	1	—	2
Falaite	2	2	1	—	1	3	2	—	—	7	6	—
Olimarao	—	—	3	1	—	1	2	—	2	—	2	—
Lamaliur	2	—	2	—	—	1	—	—	—	1	1	1
Falipi	2	3	—	—	—	—	—	1	1	—	—	—
Total	6	7	6	3	2	13	9	1	5	9	9	3

Plate 20. Several men carrying sacks of copra from the ocean side of the island to their canoe houses for drying.

spend a full day at a single task, though, so his output would equal
the number of hours expended with a yield of some ten pounds
per hour.

In the year between June, 1962, and May, 1963, the people of
Lamotrek produced between 500 and 600 sacks of copra. On each
of the three annual copra-buying visits of the trading vessel at
least 40 of the 56 adult males on the island had copra to sell. Copra
production is both seasonal—being geared to the arrival of the
trading vessel—and accomplished in a spurt of activity, rather than
a prolonged cycle of low output. This is reasonable from two points

Plate 21. Men repairing the seams of a canoe at Kulong canoe house.

of view. First, the copra which brings the highest prices is that which has been most recently produced. Second, weather factors do not always allow one to continue the drying process over a long period of time, hence it is economically more feasible to dry a large amount of copra at the same time, when the weather is good, rather than attempt to dry smaller amounts over a greater length of time.

Construction and repair of canoes and buildings is another major activity of men. Although few canoes are constructed in any one year, nearly every canoe which is used with any frequency must undergo some repairs each year and major repairs about once every year and a half. A small paddling canoe can be built by one or two men within two or three months; a large sailing canoe may take more than a year. Repair of a large canoe will take between one and two weeks depending on the number of men working and whether the seams, as well as the lashings, are renewed. There are 13 sailing canoes on Lamotrek and 23 paddling canoes. The

Plate 22. Rethatching Leibwul canoe house.

sailing canoes range in size from 14 feet up to 26 feet in length. A paddling canoe is usually only large enough to hold one or two men. At any one time 9 of the sailing canoes and 19 or more of the paddling canoes are seaworthy. March and April are the months when the general overhaul of a large canoe occurs. This is the time of the year immediately preceding intensive turtle hunting. Other small-scale repairs can be completed as necessary throughout the year. Canoe construction can be started any time during the year but seems to be more common between November and March, which comprises both the non-turtle and non-bread-fruit seasons.

House construction is infrequent but repairs, especially rethatching, occur every year or two. Rethatching does not take long since only one-half of the roof is usually renewed at a time. The thatch is gathered and woven by the residents and other lineage members; a small house requires some 300 coconut frond thatches per side, while a canoe house will require 700 or more. Thatch for the latter will be contributed by all members of the same clan plus members of other lineages which use the canoe house. When the actual thatching takes place all of the available men on the island will contribute labor and the job can be completed in two or three hours. Other house repairs occur when needed throughout the year.

Manufacture of cordage and rope and construction or repair of traps and nets, as well as other fishing equipment, are all men's work and consume a good deal of the time throughout the year. When a man has nothing more pressing to do he will usually be found in a canoe house making twine or repairing a piece of his fishing equipment.

The average work day of a man, then, is just as long as that of a woman, but there are some significant differences in labor patterns. A woman's work is more uniform. The major break in her daily activity occurs seasonally, when a shift from an emphasis on taro to breadfruit occurs. At this time her work day is somewhat shorter than it is during the rest of the year, mainly because

Plate 23. Letaugomar weaving a *tur* at Imuailap *bwogat*.

breadfruit requires so much less cultivation than taro, but also because at this time men help in the harvest of the tree product. The other activities of a woman are much the same throughout the year and are centered around cooking and weaving. A man's work day, on the other hand, is much more variable, both from day to day and from season to season. Copra, turtle hunting, breadfruit picking, and canoe repairs are all somewhat seasonal, and a man's activities must be adjusted to compensate for this. The actual number of jobs a man is responsible for is larger, hence he is not able to devote large blocks of time, as is a woman, to any one activity.

Children are assigned tasks appropriate to their sex. Up to about five or six years of age they are more or less free to play as they wish with siblings, peers, and older children who are acting as overseers. At the age of six or seven a child will begin to help adults on a more regular basis—boys accompany men fishing or in the gathering of palm sap, and girls help to harvest taro, cook, fetch water and firewood. By age 12 the boys are regular fishermen, often going out independently or in small groups to spend the morning or afternoon on the lagoon. Girls of this age will be working regularly in the taro fields, preparing food, and learning to loom-weave. More specialized tasks, such as fancy weaving among women, or canoe building, navigation, and preparation of medicine among men, will be taught following puberty as the individual shows a desire to learn them.

PATTERNS OF DISTRIBUTION AND CONSUMPTION

Food distribution is based on named homesteads and the number of inhabitants residing on each at the time of distribution. With the exception of ceremonial occasions, distribution of agricultural products does not often cross *bwogat* boundaries. The women of each homestead harvest taro from swamp holdings of that particular homestead and prepare the food for the residents. On those occasions when women from two different homesteads work together the relationship of the women (and hence the *bwogat*) is usually one of common lineage via different descent lines. Thus, the distribution which occurs will remain within the same clan and probably the same lineage.

Coconuts—the agricultural product for which men have the primary responsibility—are distributed somewhat differently. A man may harvest nuts from the trees of either his own or his wife's lineage; thus those which he provides each day for consumption by the personnel of his homestead of residence may come from the land of either or both. Similarly, when a man is obligated to contribute nuts for a ceremonial function he may take them from the trees of either lineage. In this way, a man from another island who has moved to Lamotrek following marriage has access to coconut trees even if he is unable to trace some relationship or establish ties of his own on the island. This is sometimes the case when men come from islands as far away as Truk, Sonsoral, or the Mortlocks, where the clans of the Western Carolines may be absent.

A lone man who has been fishing has the responsibility of distributing his catch on his return. His first concern is for his homestead of residence, which, if he is married, will be that of his wife. If his catch is of sufficient size he will distribute a portion to his *bwogat* of origin, the homestead of his father (if the father is no longer living at the homestead of the man's mother), and possibly to the *bwogat* of his adoptive parents if such exists.

The distribution of a catch from a communal fishing expedition, or of a catch resulting from the combined efforts of men from several different lineages, proceeds along different lines. On one such communal net drive in July of 1962, most of the able-bodied men left the island at eight o'clock in the morning in five sailing and several paddling canoes bound for the reef and channel just south of Pugue. Tagilimal and Igüfail, in different canoes, led the expedition. Tirpo rode with Tagilimal and Tachep accompanied Igüfail; both of these men are *ochang*. When all of the canoes had arrived at the channel, which is called *tauelïpukh*, Tagilimal spread his men across the north side and with some of the men in the water and some still in canoes began to drive southward across the channel toward the reef *holimel*. Igüfail had meanwhile anchored his canoe at the south end of the area and stationed his men in the water in an arc extending from the reef into the lagoon and northward. Thus, when the men of Tagilimal's team met the northernmost individuals from Igüfail's group a long semicircle was formed, with the northern and southern ends standing on the reef. Nets were then thrown into the water at both ends of the line of men and moved round the semicircle until they were joined; thus, an area some 200 or 300 yards across was enclosed. All of the men then entered the water and

Plate 24. Tagilimal and Igùfail directing a fish-trap drive on the lagoon side of the island.

fastened stones to the bottom of the coconut sennit net. When this was accomplished the net was pulled toward the reef from both ends and at the same time the men on the reef began to move toward each other. The men in the water followed the net in and cleared it from coral snags as the water became more shallow. This process continued until a complete circle of only 20 or 30 feet in diameter was formed in water three or four feet deep. Several men then took smaller nets, went inside the enclosing circle of the larger one, and removed the trapped fish. About 500 pounds of groupers, snappers, parrots, and other fish were taken in this one drive. Throughout the whole procedure many directions and comments were shouted back and forth between all the men, but the directions of Tagilimal, Igùfail, Tirpo, and Tachep were the ones with precedence. Tagilimal and Igùfail were in the water at different locations along the net and Tirpo and Tachep remained in paddling canoes, skirting behind the men from one end of the drive to the other, where they relayed directions and made suggestions.

Two other drives were made on other parts of the reef, but neither was as profitable as the first, so that by two o'clock the canoe fleet was returning to the island. The day's catch was considered extremely good and the men were in high spirits. All canoes which approach Lamotrek (and most other inhabited islands of the Western Carolines) must drop their sails and unstep their masts some

200 yards offshore as a sign of deference to the island. When this had been done and the canoes were being paddled toward the beach, several men standing on the outrigger platforms of the canoes began a *foto* dance. The *foto* dance is performed by returning fishermen when the catch has been exceptionally good; if blue-water fish are involved the dance is called *hailul*. The other men on the canoes enthusiastically cheered the chanting of the dancers, which was meant to inform the people of the island of the good catch. In response, many of the women came to the shore and countered with their own dancing and singing. As the canoes reached the beach in front of their respective canoe houses the women rapidly dispersed. The fish were collected at Urieitakh, which is Tagilimal's canoe house, where they were to be divided. When more than one of the chiefs has participated in the fishing the catch is assembled at the canoe house of the more senior man. Meanwhile the women had brought several pots of cooked breadfruit and taro for the men and left them at the side of Urieitakh before again departing, since they are not permitted to be nearby during the actual distribution.

Yangeriliel, a Hatamang man, and Mahoa, a young man of Umai's lineage, then began the actual act of distribution. The men who physically distribute the catch are not the chiefs, although the latter do have the right to decide if there is to be any variation in the usual pattern of distribution. The distributors are men of lesser status, often senior men from the junior clans or, as in this case, junior men from the senior clans. The catch was counted and sorted into three groups according to size. The chiefs and the distributors then consulted about the actual allotment, keeping in mind the number of fish available and the present population of the island (including visitors). When the number of fish is not a simple multiple of the adult population, the distribution will take place in a series of at least two steps. The first share is almost invariably allotted to the women residents of each homestead. The second share will be dependent on the number of remaining fish. It may be allocated according to the number of men, to the homestead itself, to the homesteads of the chiefs, or to visitors or regular unmarried residents of the various canoe houses. Rarely are shares made directly to children in the process of distribution. In this case Mahoa began by calling out the name of the northernmost homestead while Yangeriliel started with the southernmost. They then worked toward each other in the roll call of *bwogat*. A representative of each of the named homesteads came forward to receive the women's share as it was counted out. At this time he could correct the distributor if he felt an error had been made in his allotment. This rarely happens, but when it does he will enumerate the number of women (or men) who are to receive a share and the distributor will thus be corrected. Such errors only occur when the distributor has forgotten a visiting relative or a change in residence. The homestead representative who collects the share is often a young boy, even when an adult male is present from that homestead. A single representative may collect shares for several different homesteads if he has ties to each, and subsequently turns each share over to the appropriate *bwogat*. On this particular occasion nearly 650 pounds of fish were distributed in the following way:

1.	Lechib	30 lbs.	14.	Hapilifal	20 lbs.
2.	Hapilamahal	38½	15.	Leiho	25
3.	Olipùpù	30	16.	Iaopïl	30
4.	Imuailap	22½	17.	Iloritur	35
5.	Omaras	22	18, 19. Leomoi,		
6.	Chiligilafa	35½		Limaraorao	29½
7.	Hapalam	28	20.	Lugulior	20
8, 9.	Faligiliau,		21.	Onesh	22½
	Imùpù	37½	22.	Fairochekh	20
10.	Onïsal	12½	23.	Leihao	20
11.	Leomar	37	24.	Ralumai	7½
12.	Sabwaikh	20	25.	Peiliwer	17½
13.	Sarishe	17½	—	Ethnog., assist.	7½

The allotments amounted to between three and a half and four pounds of fish per person. Faligiliau-Imùpù and Leomoi-Limaraorao received their shares as single units, reflecting the fact that the second *bwogat* in each of these cases is an offshoot of the first.

As soon as the *bwogat* representative received the share of his homestead he left the area and carried it to the particular homestead where the women were waiting to cook it.

The distribution of turtle meat follows the same outline as that for the catch of communal fishing expeditions with the following variations. The turtles to be divided are turned on their backs and placed in shallow depressions scooped from the sand on the beach. Their flippers are cut off and while the turtles are still alive they are covered with dry palm fronds which are fired. After one or two hours the turtles are dead and the meat close to the shell roasted.

Plate 25. Men removing a turtle from the beach after roasting to begin distribution.

The turtles are pulled from the beach to the flat in front of the canoe house and opened by removing the breastplates. Two or three men work on each turtle and remove all of the meat, fat, eggs, and viscera. This is placed on nearby palm fronds which have been provided for this purpose. Several other men, usually at least one from each lineage, cut this meat into equal portions. When all of the turtles have been butchered and the meat cut up and counted, it is distributed, giving equal portions of meat, eggs, fat, and viscera to each homestead according to its population. While the main work of butchering is taking place the men of higher status, especially the chiefs, are given small cuts of meat which had been close to the shell, and hence are well roasted, to eat. The rest of the men may consume small pieces as they work. The breastplates, which are removed first, are usually given to the young boys and often young girls who are about so that they may eat the shreds of meat which have adhered. Just as in the distribution of fish, though, no

Plate 26. Distribution of turtle meat in front of Urieitakh canoe house. The head will go to Fairochekh homestead, as that is the residence of the paramount chief.

other women are allowed to be nearby while the butchering is taking place.

Those men of lower status who were actually involved in the turtle hunt will usually not participate in its subsequent distribution, although their homesteads will receive their normal shares. The long bones of the turtle, after most of the meat has been removed, are given to the canoe house from which the turtle hunters came. The meat remaining on these bones is eaten at a later time by the men who are affiliated there. The only other portion of the turtle which has a specific distribution is the head and neck, which is given to Fairochekh bwogat, the homestead of the paramount chief of Lamotrek. If more than one turtle is being butchered only one head and neck need be given to the residents of this homestead; the others are distributed as part of the total product.

The food for ceremonial feasts is distributed in much the same

way except that it will have been cooked at the individual homesteads or by the women of the different clans working together the
day before distribution is to occur. It is assembled at the point of
distribution the following day and redistributed by homestead to
the residents who have gathered for the feast. A common place
for such ceremonial distribution is at Lamïtakh. Those who attend
the feast will usually seat themselves about the area in groups
which are made up of their usual homestead residents.

The most common feast which occurs on Lamotrek is the funeral feast, prepared by the lineage of the deceased. Often the
lineage of the father of the deceased will also contribute labor and
food. All of the residents of Lamotrek will be invited to one of these
feasts and all of the taro or breadfruit which is provided will come

Plate 27. Lùmetabusho's body ready for burial, surrounded by mourners and
her children.

from the land of the above-mentioned lineages and clans. The fish which is eaten will have been caught on a fishing expedition of the previous day, manned by the men of these same lineages and any others who wish to help. The distribution and exchange of goods during and after funerals is not limited to subsistence items. The importance of the ceremony and others like it warrants a detailed discussion.

Pomai, who preceded Umai as *malübwogat* of Hapilamahal, died on the afternoon of September 10, 1962. The *shateng*, or ceremonies involved in the funeral, began immediately. Those present in the canoe house when Pomai died began wailing, and the knowledge of his death rapidly spread to all on the island. When someone is gravely ill, as Pomai had been, he is usually moved from a dwelling house into a canoe house. Here, in this larger structure, the patient can be given constant attention by his relatives, who move from their respective dwellings to stay with him for the duration

Plate 28. Men building a coffin from an old paddling canoe hull for the burial of Pomai.

of his illness. Pomai's body was bathed within an hour of his death, wrapped in *tur* and cloth, and laid out in the center of the canoe house, where it was decorated with turmeric (*rang*) and flower garlands. After the initial one or two hours of grief-stricken cries the wailing became more formalized and assumed the pattern of dirge singing. Men and women both participate in the singing of dirges, but the latter predominate. By late afternoon representatives of the other *bwogat* began to visit the canoe house to present funeral gifts and offer sympathy or participate in the dirge singing. Funeral gifts can be classified as either *tugùtug* or *paliwen*. *Tugùtug* is a normal funeral gift of *tur*, cloth, or occasionally perfume, which may be made by any lineage or descent line representatives to the lineage of the deceased. *Paliwen,* as described before, is an obligated gift made to a lineage or descent line in recognition of a gift received from that lineage. A *paliwen* offering takes the same form as a *tugùtug* (i.e., *tur* or cloth), but when it is given it is made clear to the recipient that it is *paliwen*.

On the morning after Pomai's death the men of the other *bwogat* divided into two groups for the purposes of constructing the coffin and digging the grave. The coffin was made in front of Leibwul from the hull of an old paddling canoe. When it was finished it was taken inside the canoe house and lined with *tur*, most of which had been received as *tugùtug* and *paliwen,* before the body was placed in it and the top was lashed on. The coffin was then carried to the graveyard behind the church, with the islanders following in procession, and buried.

On the morning following burial the men of the island, again in procession, each took four coconuts to Leibwul, where they were left in a pile close to the entrance. No words passed between these men and the relatives of Pomai, who were seated inside, until Fahoitip, the husband of Pomai's sister, reached out and gave Tirpo two small packages of tobacco. Tirpo tried to pass these on first to Tagilimal and then to Igùfail, but both refused to accept them (possibly because they thought there was not enough to go around). Tirpo then opened them and distributed their contents among the rest of the men.

Twenty-six of the men leaving coconuts at Leibwul took them from trees of their own lineage, 18 left nuts they had taken from the trees of their wives' lineages, and 4 provided nuts from land to which they have more distant ties. In sum, then, 192 coconuts were

Plate 29. Women preparing food for the funeral feast.

left at Leibwul to be consumed by the 20 to 25 mourners who continued to sleep there. In addition the women of each of the other *bwogat* left a small pot of cooked breadfruit or taro at the canoe house on this same day. And those homesteads on the island which owed a favor to the people of Hapilamahal continued to provide this food for a total of four days.

Four days after his death some 20 members of Pomai's lineage or affines cut the hair from their heads as a sign of mourning. Pomai's wife and daughter had shaved their heads previously, on the day of burial, and placed their hair in his grave. On this fourth day, eight of the women involved buried their hair in the graves of other deceased lineage members, but none of the men did so.

The funeral feast is supposedly held on the eighth day after

Plate 30. Preparation of an *um:* women are here arranging the fuel.

death, but in this case it did not take place until the eleventh. Preparations began September 17, when Mahoa and several women and children of the lineage started to gather coconut husks and wood for the *um* (earth oven) fires. On September 18 a sailing canoe with a crew made up of men from Hapilamahal set out for Pugue and returned with five sacks of mature coconuts to be used in cooking for the feast. On September 19 the taro (*Cyrtosperma*) to be cooked was harvested. Lefaioup, Pomai's daughter, contributed 220 of these tubers and Ilangùtamal, Pomai's sister, provided 230 from the land of her lineage. *Colocasia* was contributed by residents of homesteads who were related to Pomai by marriage, adoption, or patrilaterally; 125 of these tubers were given to Ilangùtamal and 290 to Lefaioup. Two *um* were dug the next day, one in the south at Yapùi and the other near Hapilamahal. The activities at the Yapùi *um* were presided over by a woman who was patrilaterally related to Pomai, while the northern *um* was under the direction

Plate 31. Firing the *um*.

of both Lefaioup and Ilangútamal. Lefaioup would have been more directly concerned with the southern oven if she had not been staying at Leibwul. At the same time as the ovens were being prepared two sailing canoes set out to obtain fish for the feast. One originated at Urieitakh, the northern canoe house of Tagilimal's lineage (and Pomai's subclan), and the other at Lugal, the canoe house of Lefaioup's lineage, which was manned by individuals of Iur district. The canoes returned with a total of 310 small and moderate-sized reef fish. All of the fish and most of the taro was prepared for the *um* and by nightfall it had been covered over and left to cook until the next morning.

On the afternoon of September 21 the funeral feast was held in front of Leibwul. The food had been assembled in a pile and the residents of the island were seated in small *bwogat* clusters wherever they could find shade. Mahoa, Mahomai (his younger brother), and Uromai (the younger brother of Umai) distributed a share of each type of cooked food to all the homestead groups and everyone ate.

When they were finished, Mahoa, Uromai, and Yangeriliel began to distribute the remaining cooked and uncooked food. First portions of the cooked taro were given to all *bwogat*. Then portions were given to residents who were originally from other islands (e.g., Puluwat, Satawal, etc.). What remained of the cooked food was distributed equally to the men of each of the island's canoe houses. The uncooked food (which included rice purchased from the trading ship) was distributed according to *bwogat* and also some was set aside to be taken to residents who were away on Pugue and Falaite making copra. The ceremony was concluded when tobacco was given to the men of other lineages who had helped the people of Hapilamahal in one way or another during the funeral and its subsequent feast.

As one can easily note, the funeral is an occasion when several different types of goods besides food are distributed and exchanged.

Plate 32. Men distributing the stones after they are heated so that the bundles of food may be added and covered for cooking.

I shall refer to this example, as well as several others previously mentioned, in the discussion below.

EXCHANGE AND GIFTS

With the exception of the ceremonial occasions previously mentioned, food, as such, is not often distributed beyond lineage or clan lines on Lamotrek. The dispersed land holdings associated with the *bwogat* provide each lineage with productive areas typical of all vegetation zones on the island. Thus, one lineage is not likely to have a great surplus of one commodity while lacking in another.

On Lamotrek itself the exchange of manufactured items is also likely to be more symbolic and ceremonial than necessary to insure an even distribution of goods. *Tugutug* and *paliwen, chuitibwul* (gifts made to adoptive parents), *muimuilimashang* (gift made to a chief for breaking a fishing taboo—all involve manufactured items, primarily *tur, holühol* (sennit cordage), and cloth. And all are symbolic of social and economic relationships between the two parties concerned, as the gifts themselves are not of great value. *Chüitibwul* is offered by the true parents to the couple who are adopting their child. The gift is symbolically reciprocal for the economic rights this child will have to the land and resources of the adoptive parents. When a man offers *muimuilimashang* he recognizes that the reef, lagoon, and their resources are owned by the chiefs. All men have equal rights to fish the reef and lagoon of Lamotrek, but, as Map 10 shows, control of these areas is divided among the chiefly clans. The heads of these clans have the right to limit net fishing and prohibit all fishing in their respective areas when a senior member of their clan dies (although the latter prohibition has not been imposed since conversion to Christianity). The clan chief involved will inform the men of the island of his decision by placing poles in the reef which have a coconut frond *pan-nu* taboo sign affixed. Any man who fishes this area in defiance of the taboo will have his canoe confiscated by the chief when he returns to the island. Confiscation is accomplished when another frond called *mashang* is tied to the prow of the vessel. The fisherman must then offer *muimuilimashang* to the chief before he is allowed to resume fishing. In doing so, he acknowledges that it is only with the permission of the chiefs that he and all other men are allowed to exploit the resources of the reef and lagoon.

Paliwen is an offering made by one lineage to another which acknowledges that certain real property exploited by the former is residually owned by the latter.[2] The decision to award a land gift is not one which is easily reached, for the productive potential of the land for several generations may be involved. Land gifts are often symptomatic of other alterations within the society and a resulting need or desirability for a redistribution of land beyond individual clan lines. Previously cited examples have shown that on the one hand such changes, in the form of lineage and subclan expiration, were why Lefaioup turned some of her land over to Sauwel, and on the other hand were why Sarishe reached independent status, when its mother lineage reached such a size as to warrant fission. *Paliwenübwogat* is thus made to the residual owners as long as the resident owners wish to remain and exploit the holdings. *Paliwenülü* and *paliwenümai*, as their names imply, are offerings made to residual owners respectively for the gift of a coconut palm and a breadfruit tree. The occasions when one would transfer exploitative ownership of a tree are more varied than those for similar transfer of land ownership. I have records of 103 coconut trees which were given by one lineage to another; the reasons for these gifts can be classified as follows: patrilateral gifts (i.e., given by a man or some other member of his lineage to his children), 34; gifts made to a spouse, 28; presented in recognition of an adoptive tie, 11; given as payment for some type of favor received (especially medical aid), 10; given as objects of friendship, 8; exchanged (i.e., two men decided to trade trees for one or another reason), 4; given for unknown or forgotten reasons, 8. As long as *paliwen* is offered the recipient lineage may keep the tree for as long as it lives.

Thus, the majority of manufactured objects which are exchanged between the inhabitants of Lamotrek are symbolic items which refer to the exchange of real property, or the economic exploitation rights granted by one party to another in areas or objects owned by the former. The outstanding and only important exception to the above generalization is the canoe, which is a special type of property. Exchange of canoes is more restricted and residual title in one is not recognized. As a gift, there are only two instances when a canoe crosses clan or subclan boundaries: (1) *Gift to spouse.* A man may build a canoe which he gives to his wife and her lineage.

---

[2] Residual ownership among residents of the Truk Islands has been discussed by Goodenough (1951:34).

Since the canoe has not had established ownership within his own lineage he need not obtain permission from the other senior members of his lineage. Such an individual will usually build the canoe because his wife's lineage has a shortage of such craft. In doing so he will have access to a vessel which he can use in contributing to the support of his wife, children, and their lineage. (2) *Gift to children*. A canoe gift will also cross clan boundaries when a man passes one from his own lineage to one of his children, usually a son. This form of patrilateral gift will need the approval of the man's lineage; thus, it will only be a senior man of the lineage who will attempt to make such a gift.

In both of the above cases no *paliwen* reciprocity is necessary, for the ownership of a canoe carries no idea of residual ownership as does the ownership of real property and trees. This difference in property classification may lie in the nature of the gift as either movable or immovable property. In Chapter 3 it was said that residence on a piece of land and/or exploitation of a particular plot or tree are important considerations if a claim to ownership is made and the plot or tree has changed hands in the past. *Paliwen* can be demanded because the ownership history of a piece of land or a tree can be clearly demonstrated by its location: either its proximity to other owned plots or trees or the political district in which it is

Plate 33.   Men carrying coconuts as gifts to Kulong canoe house, where someone lies ill.

found and from which it cannot be moved. The ownership history of a movable piece of property may be more difficult to trace or prove. When canoe ownership is transferred the craft may be completely removed from the lineage land, the district, or the island. There is no question of ownership reverting to the original lineage when the object is no longer exploited by the recipient lineage, both because the item may not be in the district or even on the island and because canoes are only abandoned when they become unseaworthy. The *paliwen* is a symbol of specific occasions which is transmitted promptly by a co-resident and which is meaningless and impossible to provide by a resident of another island who will not be present when a *paliwen* occasion arises.

In conclusion, exchange for the purpose of obtaining food and manufactured objects is not common among residents and between clans on Lamotrek, primarily because the holdings of one are similar to the holdings of any other. This type of exchange and trade does occur, though, and is a very important facet of economic and political life on an inter-island level. The resources of one island are often richer in particular goods—either natural or manufactured —than those of a neighbor. Thus, exchange of surplus for scarcity is a primary reason behind inter-island voyages and, I believe, a fundamental reason for the existence and maintenance of inter-island political, economic, and religious ties. I shall discuss these points in the chapters to follow.

5

Religion

In 1962-63 there were no non-Christian residents on Lamotrek. Since observation of most indigenous religious practices was not possible and informants were reluctant to talk about traditional religious beliefs, the range of data gathered concerning this topic is limited. This reticence may pass with time, as conversion on Lamotrek, Elato, and Satawal is quite recent, but because of it I will not try to present a complete picture of pre-Christian beliefs. Burrows and Spiro (1953:207-43) and Lessa (1961a, 1962a) have each discussed the religious organization of neighboring Western Caroline atolls which are quite similar to Lamotrek. These authors can be consulted for more detailed accounts. In this chapter I will only discuss those features of religious belief and activity which have direct relevance to socioeconomic organization on an intra- and inter-island level.

BENEVOLENT AND MALEVOLENT GHOSTS

Belief System

The term *yalus* on Lamotrek is applied to all gods, spirits, and ghosts. *Yalus* are classified only in terms of malevolence or benevolence and by areas of abode—sky, land, and sea. Lessa (1961a:15) noted that the celestial spirits of Ulithians did not often enter into the affairs of humans as they were primarily objects of mythology. This same statement can be made concerning the creation and

114

Plate 34. Young women doing a sitting dance while Isïpito and an older woman ceremonial offer gifts over the heads of related dancers. Anyone who accepts these gifts wishes the dancer good fortune.

supercasual spirits of Lamotrek, most of which are the same as those on Ulithi. The core of Lamotrekan religious belief, as Lessa discussed for Ulithi, concerns the lesser spirits of the sky, sea, and ancestor ghosts.[1]

At death the soul (*ngül*) of the deceased becomes a *yalus*. These ghosts are divided into two large categories: those of the sky or air (*yalusülang*) and those of the sea (*yalusütat*). The former are predominantly benevolent and the latter primarily malevolent, although a further detailed division is said to exist among *yalusütat*. The *yalusütat*, so one informant stated, were divided into "good" and "bad" groups, each of which had armies of warriors which fought against each other. For most souls the factor which determined whether or not it became a good or bad ghost was the influence exerted upon it by other ghosts at the time of death and shortly thereafter. One factor which weighed heavily against an individual soul's chance of becoming a good ghost was determined by his mode of death. A person who died as a result of an accident (e.g., drowning, falling from a tree, etc.) or a woman who died when pregnant or during childbirth was most likely to become a malevolent ghost. Evil ghosts were the main cause of sickness. Burrows

---

[1] In religion, as well as many other cultural characteristics, ceremonial practices often are greatly similar to those of Truk, while the same occasions on Ulithi bear greater resemblance to Yapese behavior.

and Spiro (1953:207-43) have discussed the function of evil ghosts
in Carolinian atoll religion at some length. It should be emphasized,
though, that good or benevolent *yalus* were of equal importance in
Lamotrekan religion.

Most homesteads—and every lineage *bwogat*—had a shrine dedicated to the ghosts of the lineage. Such a shrine was most often
found inside the main dwelling house of the homestead, but if the
ghost were of island-wide importance a separate structure might be
constructed elsewhere on lineage land. A small shrine usually con-
sisted of a *hurùhur* (a round stick some four feet long used in
dancing and at one time in warfare) which hung from the roof of
the house. A bottle of coconut oil was suspended from one end and
flower garlands often hung on the other. A larger shrine would
include woven *tur*, turmeric, and offerings of food. Whereas evil
ghosts brought sickness and death, benevolent ghosts, to whom
shrines were dedicated, often provided curative knowledge or performed other acts helpful to man.

Ceremonies and Possession

The basic organization of funerals, of which Pomai's was an
example, has changed little as a result of conversion to Christianity
in 1953. In pre-Christian times, though, burial could occur either
on land or at sea. For the purpose of sea burial the body was
simply wrapped in *tur* and a mat, weighted with stones, and trans-
ported to the burial area via canoe. The two general areas in which
sea burials took place were to the north and south of Lamotrek.
The area to the north was associated with malevolent deaths and
evil *yalus*. Certain precautions were taken during the funeral of a
person who had suffered a malevolent death in an effort to prevent
his returning as an evil *yalus*. While the body was lying in state
at the canoe house all of the adult men would gather outside at
sundown. There they would decorate themselves with strips of
immature coconut leaves (*ubwut*), which are used in most religious
and magical ceremonies, and some would carry conch-shell horns.
The men would then proceed from one end of the island to the
other blowing the horns, reciting chants, and striking the walls,
floors, and rafters of all houses and canoe houses on the island in
an attempt to drive all malevolent ghosts off the island so that they
would not gain possession of the soul of the accident victim. The

women and children would remain inside the canoe house during the ceremony and were not supposed to look out. The body would then be prepared for sea burial, since burial on land was not permitted after this type of death, and taken in a canoe beyond the reef north of the island. In this area of the open sea it would be dropped overboard while the men of the canoe would shout after it that it should go down. They would watch as it sank beneath the surface, and if the body descended from sight without hesitation this was interpreted as a good omen. If, on the other hand, it hesitated as it sank or partially rose again before being lost to sight, the omen was bad and it was quite probable that the soul had been taken by malevolent ghosts and would, in turn, become one too. Before the practice of sea burial was abandoned the open sea south of Lamotrek was also a burial area. The south, though, was reserved for individuals who had died normal deaths and hence were least likely to become evil ghosts. Informants said that chiefs were buried far to the south—probably around ten miles from the island.

Benevolent *yalus* often maintained direct communication with living people through mediums or *waliyalus* (canoe or vehicle of the *yalus*). An individual who was recognized as a medium was such for a particular ghost who was often, but not always, a deceased member of the medium's lineage or clan. Women made up a large percentage of the island's mediums and it seems that they were frequently mediums for one of their own dead children. A ghost would often tell its medium of imminent sickness, suggest preventative or curative medicines, or notify the whole population via the medium of some impending phenomenon (e.g., a storm or the arrival of a canoe or ship).

Possession by a benevolent ghost could take the form of marriage if the medium concerned were an unmarried female. In these instances the ghost would naturally not be of the same clan as the medium. At the time of this study there were three remembered instances of such marriages. One occurred between a medium from one of the southern homesteads and a *yalus* who, as a consequence, would bring fish to her dwelling during the night. In return the woman would prepare food for him which she would leave overnight for his consumption. In another case a woman from the island's middle district, who was a leper, awoke one night and told the other members of the house that she had been contacted by a *yalus* who wished to marry her. On several subsequent occasions the ghost revisited her and each time she informed the other residents of this. This ghost told her that as a result of the marriage she would bear him ten children. Before the marriage actually occurred, though, the woman was taken to the lazaretto on Tinian by the American administrative authorities. When she eventually returned to Lamotrek communication with the ghost was never re-established. The final instance I shall cite of attempted marriage with a ghost occurred on Elato. In this case a medium was contacted by a ghost who said that he wished to marry the medium's daughter. The girl, though, ignored the proposal and married a man from Lamotrek. Within a year of their marriage the man died. The girl married again and her second husband also died. The girl's third marriage was to the brother of her second husband. The medium reminded her daughter of the ghost's proposal and told her that she had better convert to Christianity in order to avoid the further displeasure of this ghost. She followed this advice and her husband remains in good health.

Direct communication with malevolent ghosts is of a more diffuse nature. They possess no permanent mediums but often make themselves known to individuals or groups by throwing stones, whispering, or whistling. One woman on Elato was slapped in the face by a ghost, while another on Lamotrek, whom the people say is insane, has bruises on her arms caused by evil *yalus*. One of my informants recalled that he and his sister were seated by their homestead dwelling several years ago when they heard the whispering of a malevolent ghost. The woman suggested that her brother offer a cigarette to the *yalus*. He did this, the smoke was seen to be inhaled by the ghost, and he was thus placated and left. *Yalusütat* may also take direct reprisals against individuals who offend them. Fishermen must not injure and leave either fish or turtles, but must pursue their prey until taken. If a wounded fish or turtle escapes the fisherman, he must, when he returns to the island, consume a prophylactic medicine in order to counteract the anger of the *yalus*.

It is not   usual for the influence of a ghost to extend beyond the life-span of its medium. When one medium dies and is replaced by someone else, that new medium will be spokesman for her own ghost, not for her predecessor's.

PATRON SPIRITS

Belief System

Another group of *yalus* are the patrons of particular endeavors
and their assistance is sought by practitioners of these activities to
insure success. Navigation, with Yalulawei as patron spirit, and
canoe building, with Semeligarara and Selangi as patrons, are the
two outstanding examples. These are spirits whose aid to craftsmen
is not short-lived. They are *yalus* with permanent positions within
the belief system. When one learns navigation or boatbuilding one
also learns the rituals necessary to gain the aid of the appropriate
patron. There is no spirit possession when dealing with patron
yalus; all navigators and canoe builders have access to and can
seek the help of their patron. *Yalus* such as this lend aid in endeavors which are primarily the responsibility of the relevant crafts-
man. They do not affect random events such as ghosts of mediums.

Ceremonies

The foremost ceremony involving a patron spirit occurs when a
navigator (*pelu*) consecreates a weather effigy or *hos*; there are
several names for this effigy, but this is the most common and
refers to the sting-ray spines which protrude from its base. At the
completion of a navigator's training he will seek the aid of Yalulawei
for his future voyages. And the weather effigy is an important item
in the navigator's paraphernalia, for with it he will ward off bad
weather during his voyages and turn storms away from his island
of residence. The effigy can be carved by anyone with woodworking
ability. From two to six sting-ray spines are bound to its base and
overlaid with coral cement. When completed, the navigator takes
the effigy to a particular coconut tree, which may have been given
to him by the individual from whom he learned navigation and
which is located near his canoe house. Here he recites a chant and
Yalulawei is asked to protect the navigator through the effigy
wherever he travels. The *hos* can now be taken on a canoe and
when not in use is kept at the canoe house. It is never taken to a
dwelling house.

Navigators who have gained the aid of Yalulawei might use the
effigy and their knowledge for purposes of sorcery (*saoso*), but if
death is brought about by a sorcerer he, too, would die as a result

Plate 35. Yoromai carving a *hos* on Elato to be used by a navigator.

of his activities.[2] *Saoso* can also be performed by women, but naturally they would not make use of navigational lore. In the early 1940's, for example, a woman of Elato allowed several young girls to pick flowers for garlands from her land, but she warned them that they were not to take them all. The following day, though, she discovered that someone had returned without permission and taken the last of the blossoms. She asked the girls about this, but none would admit the theft. The shrubs involved had been grow-

---

[2] One informant mentioned that the sorcerers of Ifaluk were especially feared until recent years. This comment has some relevance to the exchange which recently occurred between W. A. Lessa and M. E. Spiro (*American Anthropologist* 63:817 ff.), as it was the informant who introduced Ifaluk into the conversation.

ing near the taro swamp and upon investigation the woman found a footprint of the offender nearby. She removed the section of earth with this imprint and took it to her house, where she performed *saoso* with it, the exact nature of which was unknown to my informant. As a result, in 1948 one of the girls who had been involved came down with filariasis of the leg. She then admitted that she had been the offender.

Love magic—which some informants said was practiced on Lamotrek while others denied it—apparently could also be performed by either sex. A woman would try to attract a particular man to herself through a ceremony carried out in the taro swamp and which involved decorating herself with *ubwut* and coconut oil. A man, on the other hand, might attempt similar magic while in a canoe on the lagoon. In all of the above cases magic seems to be effective when carried out in the domain appropriate to the sex of the magician. Undoubtedly, though, the navigator stands as the most powerful supernatural manipulator on Lamotrek. He can affect the weather, perform rituals to abrogate the maleffects of breaking a taboo, he is usually skilled at divination and, if necessary, sorcery.

INTER-ISLAND GHOSTS AND SPIRITS

Even though certain greater celestial spirits are widespread in the mythology of the Western Carolines (although their influence is slight in day-to-day affairs), and the patron spirits mentioned above are appealed to by the residents and craftsmen of most of the islands of this area, most of the benevolent and malevolent ghosts are localized or restricted in effectiveness to particular islands. An important exception to this generalization, though, exists in the case of the ghosts Maresùpa, Ilef, and Rongala.

In the recent past (pre-1953) there were ghost-house shrines for these three *yalus* on Lamotrek. The house of Maresùpa and his Lamotrek medium were found at Olipùpù *bwogat*. Chiligilafa homestead was the location of the ghost-house of Ilef, where a woman acted as his medium. And finally, the house of Rongala was at Hafiliang, where a male medium resided. The distinguishing characteristic of these *yalus* was that all originated not on Lamotrek but on Ulithi atoll. My informant stated that the clan affiliations of these ghosts (when they were still living) were not known.

Thus, they were not necessarily related to the particular medium who dealt with each. These *yalus* were adopted by the Lamotrekans when Ulithians who visited the island convinced individual Lamotrekans that the ghosts should be paid proper respect on this island as well as on Ulithi. The informant said that because the Ulithians "were chiefs," their suggestions were followed. The year when these ghosts first were adopted on Lamotrek is not remembered, but at least Maresùpa was known on the island in 1909 when Krämer visited here (Krämer 1937:139). As noted in Chapter 1, the supra-island power of Yapese magicians and spirits was one factor which maintained inter-island ties. For if tribute were not paid, reprisals, which in one form magically caused typhoons, might be taken by the Yapese. On the other hand, the Yapese could be called upon to perform magic beneficial to the outer islands, as when ceremonies were carried out to increase the number of fish in the lagoon. Renowned magicians were not neces-

Plate 36. Yapi, a senior *pelu* (navigator), demonstrating the use of a *hos* in weather magic.

sarily limited to islands of higher status, however. After the typhoon of 1958, for example, a Satawalese magician was asked to carry out certain rites which it was hoped would insure the rapid recovery of the agricultural areas on Lamotrek. Undoubtedly, then, the knowledge that spirits and magicians did have inter-island power played a part in the acceptance of the three Ulithian *yalus* on Lamotrek, for Ulithi, it will be remembered, is an island of much superior status to Lamotrek, and it would not be wise to insult either the Ulithians or their ghosts.

SUMMARY

The way in which a Lamotrekan thinks of the supernatural world is in many ways a reflection of the conception he has of his own social organization. The duality of the social structure is mirrored by that of the supernatural—malevolent and benevolent, sea and sky, male and female. And again, the *pelu,* who is a man highly respected for his technical ability, is the individual who is most experienced in dealing with the supernatural. The *pelu's* knowledge is essential if inter-island voyages are to be made, and the function of inter-island *yalus* would suggest that inter-island organizational ties are also well developed.

6

Inter-Island Communication:
Concepts and Technology

THE SEA AND THE NAVIGATOR

If the degree of isolation of a given island is measured in terms of its absolute distance from another contrasted with the navigational knowledge and sailing skill possessed by its inhabitants, then the Caroline Islands under discussion must be considered among the least isolated of the world.

The sea is more than a resource area to the people of the Western Carolines; it is also a means for communication and thus not an insurmountable barrier. The vocabulary of Lamotrekese reflects this, and the vocabulary can be said to reflect categories of thinking. The open sea—i.e., those areas where no islands are visible— is called *metau*. A navigator who is traveling between two known islands would not refer to the sea around him as *metau*, however, even when he is out of sight of land. For the sea which lies between islands is individually named. For example, when traveling between Lamotrek and Satawal one is on Uoirekh, but the sea to the south, where no known islands lie, is *metau*. Map 11 lists the named sea-lanes which lie between the islands in the area of Lamotrek, while Table X is a nearly complete list of the sea-lanes for the whole of the Western Carolines. To the navigator the sea-lane is a known area. One is as sure to reach his destination if he does not stray from this lane as he is sure of reaching a destination by

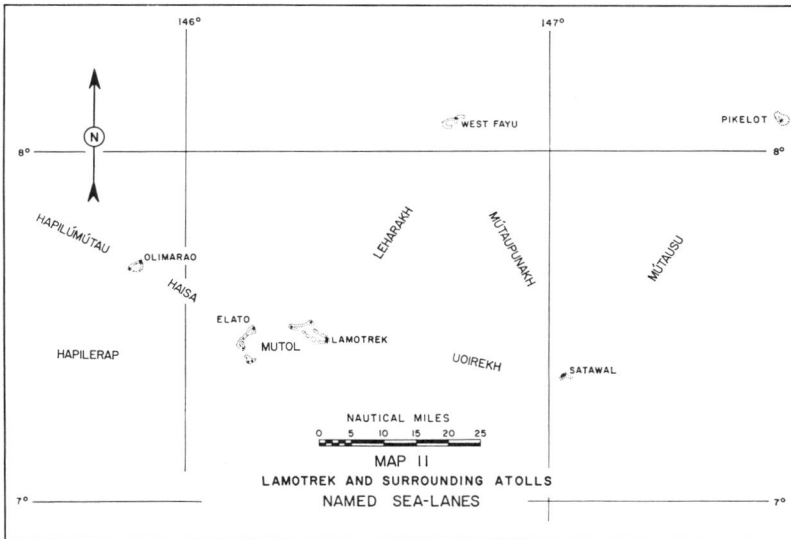

MAP 11
LAMOTREK AND SURROUNDING ATOLLS
NAMED SEA-LANES

following a known path on his home island. It is only when one wanders from the sea-lane into the *metau* that one becomes lost and disoriented. This image of the open sea suggests the regulative principle which is the basis for the ordering of space for the Lamotrekan, whether the space involved be on the island, in anatomy, construction, or navigation. The spatial ordering of the island is manifest in the division into districts, which has been discussed in Chapter 3.

TABLE X. Named Sea-Lanes of the Western Caroline Islands

Islands	Sea-Lane	Islands	Sea-Lane
Guam-Gaferut	Mùtau-uol	Ifaluk-Elato	Hapilerap
Yap-Ulithi	Mùtaurupal	Elato-Olimarao	Haisa
Ulithi-Sorol	Mùtaupengakh	Olimarao-Faraulep	Hapilùmùtau
Ulithi-Fais	Mùtaumarfach	Lamotrek-Satawal	Uoirekh
Yap-Ngulu	Chumahos (?)	Lamotrek-Pikhailo	Leharakh
Ngulu-Palau	Mùtaumal	Satawal-Pikhailo	Mùtaupunakh
Faraulep-Woleai	Faligùmatar	Satawal-Pikh	Mùtausu
Woleai-Eauripik	Mùtaulìbwul	Fais-Faraulep	Falùmùhol
Woleai-Ifaluk	Faliorùma	Fais-Eauripik	Hapilamahal
Faraulep-Ifaluk	Mùtaupugakh	Sorol-Earuipik	Gilùmar

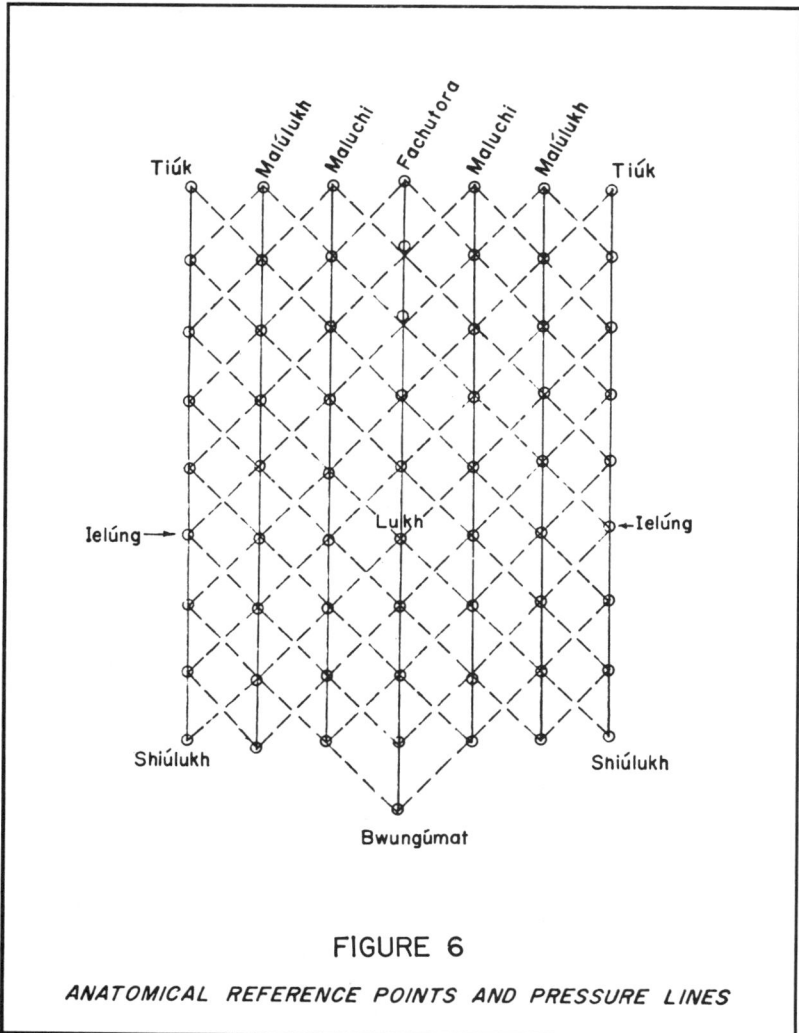

FIGURE 6

ANATOMICAL REFERENCE POINTS AND PRESSURE LINES

In anatomy the trunk is thought of as being divided by six parallel lines, three to each side of the spine, which is itself represented by a central line (Figure 6). Each of the six lines has nine significant points upon it, while the spinal line has ten. The sixth point from the top on this latter is called *lukh* or center (it falls just above the navel). Thus, there are 64 significant points of reference on this part of the body. When effecting a cure through massage—a common method on Lamotrek—pressure is applied at one of these points and directed along the vertical or diagonal lines which pass from point to point. The basis of the anatomical model, then, is a grid system of parallel and intersecting lines where the significant reference points are found at the points of intersection.

The carpenter or canoe builder (*sennap*) is a man second in prestige only to the navigator. Measurements in the construction of the Lamotrekan canoe hull (which is described by Krämer 1937:93-94) are controlled by the *sennap* with the use of measuring lines of either sennit twine—which once had magical significance— or a strip taken from the central spine of a coconut frond. Many of the crucial measurements of the canoe are derived from an initial measurement by folding and refolding the measuring line at its mid-point (*lukh*) until the required length is reached. This method of "halving" is in opposition to a system which would depend on the multiplication of a set unit to the required length. The uniformity in thought in all these fields is that of duality (or triadic duality) and lineality. The inter-island sea-lane of the navigator is a similar concept. Its lineality is obvious, though whether it includes a triadic/dualistic division is not clear from the information I have at hand. During a voyage to Satawal it did not occur to me to question the *pelu* about any subdivision or *lukh* of Uoirekh. Nevertheless, as Gladwin (1962:8-9) has also suggested in his discussion of Trukese cognitive processes, the navigator must be continually aware of his position, so that he knows the times and places where tacking is necessary. It is quite probable that the navigator's image of the seaway, under these circumstances, is subdivided—possibly at named intervals.

Navigational techniques and astronomical knowledge have been described in some detail for the Western and Central Carolines by Krämer (1937:272-77) and Goodenough (1953). As exemplified by the discussion in Chapter 5, the corpus of knowledge of a navigator includes not only the mechanics of sailing, but also a whole range of supernatural knowledge. Because of the prestige associated with this individual it is usual for most chiefs to seek training as a *pelu* so that their status position will be undisputed in all spheres. In 1962-63 there were five *pelu* of recognized standing on

Plate 37. A *pelu* directing an inter-island voyage, seated on the mid-bench of the canoe.

Lamotrek, two on Elato, and at least eight on Satawal. Navigation is usually learned from either one's father or one's mother's brother. And often such instruction will necessitate that the apprentice take up residence on another island where the *pelu* lives. If the navigator is unrelated to the potential apprentice he could refuse instruction, but if he accepts he will receive several gifts from the student and his lineage at the end of the training period. When the student is closely related to his teacher no sizable gift will be given, but the student will at least hold a feast for his instructor which will serve the dual purposes of repaying him for his services and signifying the end of his training.

One can seek training as a navigator at almost any age after 19 or 20. In 1962 a man on Elato who was in his early 40's was training under a *pelu* of Satawal who only visited Elato once every six months. He had been under instruction for several years and would probably continue to study for several more before reaching *pelu* status. At the other extreme, a young man of Satawal, who was yet in his mid-20's, had already achieved the position of *pelu*. The importance of the navigator can, in part, be illustrated by the number and frequency of inter-island canoe voyages. The number of these voyages with Lamotrek as the focus is noted in Table XI, and, as suggested here, long-distance canoe travel is dependent on seasonal variations in winds and storms as well as

TABLE XI.

A. Inter-Island Canoe Voyages

			To:		
From:	Lamotrek	Elato	Satawal	Woleai	Pulusuk
Lamotrek		30	—	—	—
Elato	9		—	—	—
Satawal	10	8		2	?
Woleai	—	—	—		—
Pulusuk	1	1	2	—	

B. Voyages Terminating at Lamotrek

						Month						
From:	5	6	7	8	9	10	11	12	1	2	3	4
Elato	2	1	—	1	1	—	1	—	—	—	2	1
Satawal	2	2	—	1	1	—	—	—	—	—	3	1
Pulusuk	1	—	—	—	—	—	—	—	—	—	—	—

C. Voyages Originating on Lamotrek

						Month						
To:	5	6	7	8	9	10	11	12	1	2	3	4
Elato	4	5	2	5	2	1	1	1	4	1	—	4
Olimarao	—	3	—	—	1	3	—	2	—	2	—	—
Lamaliur	—	2	—	—	1	—	—	—	1	1	1	2

on the economic factors already mentioned in Chapter 4. The table also shows that long-distance travel is more frequently undertaken by navigators of Satawal than by those of either Lamotrek or Elato. In part this reflects the relative capabilities of the *pelu* on the respective islands. In addition, though, the status ranking of the islands cannot be ignored as a factor which accounts for the greater number of Satawal canoes visiting Lamotrek than vice versa. Elato, because of its small population, is the point of origin for few voyages. A true picture of long-distance travel cannot be gained, however, by simply looking at the statistics of a single year. In 1960, for example, two canoes sailed from Lamotrek to Woleai. In 1961 a single canoe traveled to Truk. And in 1962-63, the period when this field work was carried out, two navigators canceled plans for voyages to Woleai and Truk because of the ethnographer's presence. Other evidence indicates that long-distance canoe travel in the past was even more extensive (and probably more frequent) than it is now. The last remembered voyage to Ulithi by a Lamotrek canoe occurred some 50 years ago. Voyages to Guam are known to have occurred but are not remembered by any navigators now living. The availability of steamship travel to these more distant islands since the arrival of foreign powers has resulted in trips of greater frequency, safety, and speed. Direct ship travel from Lamotrek to Truk is not possible, though, and the voyage to Woleai is not so hazardous as to lead to the abandoning of these routes by *pelu*.

THE CANOE BUILDER AND THE CANOE

Although less prestige is attached to the role of the *sennap* than to that of *pelu*, it remains as an important field of specialization. Indeed, the *pelu* depends on the canoe builder and master carpenter for his craft. In 1962-63 there were seven accomplished *sennap* on Lamotrek, three on Elato, and about a dozen on Satawal.[1] The canoe-building techniques practiced on these three islands are much the same today as Krämer (1937:91-106) described them in 1909. With the exception of steel-bladed construction tools and the canvas sail on the completed craft, no foreign materials are utilized. The canoe keel section is hewed from a single tree—usually

---

[1] My figures for Satawal are often less precise than those for Lamotrek or Elato owing to the fact that I was only able to spend a short time there.

Plate 38. Taro adzing a plank for canoe repair. (The tattoos on his leg are traditional representations of porpoises.)

breadfruit—and the gunwales are built up from this section by butting additional adzed planks against it. Breadfruit-sap glue and thinly trimmed coconut husks are placed between the butted planks for strength and a minimum of leakage. The planks are sewn together with coconut sennit twine and the holes through which the twine passes are filled with coral lime cement. The outrigger and counterbalance platform are tightly lashed together and the former is tied to the hull while the latter is held in place by its own weight. All rigging is made of sennit rope of varying sizes. With the exception of the sail, then, little efficiency would be gained by utilizing purchased materials of foreign manufacture. And any efficiency possibly gained (e.g., in using marine putty or glue) would be offset by the comparatively large financial outlay for such goods.

As previously stated, there were 13 ocean-going canoes and 23 paddling canoes on Lamotrek. At least nine of the former were seaworthy. The largest of these was 26 feet long and the smallest 14 feet. Elato had two ocean-sailing canoes, one of which was destroyed by high seas in 1962. The other was about 18 or 19 feet

Plate 39. An old man making sennit twine.

long. I did not make a count of paddling canoes, but doubt whether there were more than 10 on the island. Satawal had 14 ocean-going canoes with several others under construction. Paddling canoes numbered about 30. The largest Satawal canoe was 28 feet long and 5 feet from bottom of keel to top of gunwale amidship. This was the largest canoe I saw in the Carolines. Five of the other Satawal canoes approached this one in size, but breadfruit trees from which canoes like these can be constructed are not often available on most islands. Between March, 1962, and June, 1963, only two new canoes were built on Lamotrek, both of which were small paddling craft. During this same period one paddling canoe was built on Elato. Satawal, on the other hand, had four sailing canoes under construction and an equal number of one- or two-man paddling canoes. In part, this reflects the greater importance of ocean-going craft on this island, since the Satawalese depend on ocean fishing and gathering from neighboring islands more than do the inhabitants of either Lamotrek or Elato. In addition, though, canoe building is more frequent on

Satawal because that island has greater stores of breadfruit timber than are usually found on atolls.

A lineage or clan may obtain a canoe in one of two general ways. First, if there is a *sennap* in the lineage he may be asked, or himself decide, to build one. The canoe then belongs to the lineage and may be used by all members. Second, if there is no *sennap* in the lineage, the lineage may contract an established canoe builder outside its ranks to construct the craft. In this case the lineage will usually provide the materials and at the completion of the job pay the *sennap* for his labor. Either of the above methods may involve only the inhabitants of a single island or, just as often, the residents of two different islands. Since neither clans nor subclans are necessarily localized on one island it is possible that a branch of one's own subclan, found on another island, either has a more accomplished canoe builder or a larger store of raw materials to draw upon. Thus, a *sennap* of this branch may be asked to undertake the construction. As an alternative, though, if the subclan has no *sennap* it is more usual for a lineage to approach an individual on the same island rather than seek a non-kinsman from a neighboring island. In part, this is because canoe construction requires a long period of time (perhaps more than a year), and it is not considered wise to contract such a long-term project with a non-kinsman who does not reside on the same island. It would be more

Plate 40. Mahoa and Reieg adzing a canoe prow.

usual, under these circumstances, to buy an already completed canoe rather than contract to build a new one. In all instances observed on Lamotrek where a completed canoe had been purchased by one lineage from another, this transaction had taken place between islands, either Lamotrek and Satawal or Lamotrek and Puluwat. Although this is not a rule for such exchanges, it seems to be a logical development. A lineage usually will only buy a completed canoe when there is immediate need of one: when the time involved in building one would result in a long delay and consequent economic loss. The most frequent occasion of such immediate need follows a severe tropical storm or typhoon, when the canoes of the lineage have been destroyed. In this case, if one wishes a seaworthy craft he will seek one on a neighboring island which has either weathered the storm with little damage or has completely escaped it. (I shall consider the details of such an inter-island transaction in Chapter 7.) For it is only during an emergency such as this that one lineage would put pressure on another to sell a completed canoe; seaworthy craft are not held in surplus by lineages on any island. And on other occasions the need for a canoe is not so urgent that it cannot be built within the lineage or contracted to be built without.

SUMMARY

This chapter has discussed two important technological spheres of knowledge and achievement necessary for the establishment and maintenance of inter-island ties, as well as the subsistence exploitation of the environment. Navigation and canoe building are directly tied to the environment, the first to the sea and the second to the resources of the land. The knowledge and material results of both are transmitted along lines established for other material and nonmaterial possessions within Western Carolinian culture, either as concerns a single island or between islands and corporate groups. Both of these spheres of knowledge continue to have important economic, political, and religious implications as is reflected today by the number of practicing specialists and the eagerness with which the knowledge of crafts is sought. The description also suggests that the total socioeconomic system within which these individuals function is of supra-island level.

7

Inter-Island Socioeconomic Ties

When questioned, inter-island voyagers will usually provide a multiplicity of reasons for making a trip, but economic exchange, whether stated or not, almost invariably occurs between such travelers and the inhabitants of the islands visited. Kinship and political structure as well as economic organization are involved, however, so it is best when discussing ties between islands to emphasize the context of supra-island commerce.

ECONOMIC AND KIN TIES

Barter Exchange

Long-distance voyages, and particularly those beyond the region of former Yapese control, are most often initiated for economic reasons. The pre-contact expeditions to Guam and present-day trips to Truk are examples of such. In 1961, for instance, Umai sailed to Truk via Pikhailo (West Fayu), Pikh (Pikelot), Puluwat, Pulap, and Namonuito. His primary reason for going to Truk was trade, but he also had close kin on Puluwat whom he wished to visit. Whenever possible these voyages are carried out by island-hopping even if some of the islands—as Pikhailo and Pikh in this case—are not in direct line with the destination. Umai, as well as those who accompanied him, carried *tur, holühol* (cordage), and tobacco as primary trade goods. They hoped to obtain steel wiring (used for fish spears), *rang* (turmeric), *tügakh* (shell belts worn by women),

135

and such other manufactured goods found on Truk, where a trading post is located. On distant islands such as Truk, it is unusual for Lamotrekans to find kin even of common clan status. Exchange, under these circumstances, is in the form of immediate transactions. The canoe in question would arrive at Truk with a definite number of items to trade and when it left it would return with the objects gained plus any untraded capital.

Bargaining or haggling is not a part of economic exchange among the Western Carolinians. The comparative value of exchange items is well established so there is little or no difficulty in measuring the return one will make for goods received. For example, one *tur* equals four 100-fathom hanks of *holühol* in value; one medium-sized *tügakh* equals five *tur;* and the value of foreign goods is measured on the basis of one *tur* equaling four or five dollars. Among the Western Carolinians, then, just as among the Trukese of which Goodenough (1951:56-59) speaks, the introduction of money has not upset the economic system; the money and introduced products have simply been incorporated into a system of established comparative values.

Simple barter could take place between individuals from any two islands, but it is least likely to occur between islands which have close political and kinship ties. For just as in the case of intra-island exchange discussed previously, trade rarely occurs across clan or subclan lines since each kin group has access to the full range of economic goods. In this particular situation, where subclans as well as clans are not restricted to a single island, inter-island trade can easily be carried out within the same kin group. This exchange usually takes one of the forms listed below.

Contractual Exchange

This is one of the most common types of exchange which occurs between Lamotrek and her neighboring islands. Arranged exchange is the direct result of a request. An individual on one island will request—in person or via a message—some particular item from a kinsman of another island. On this basis, Lamotrek men often ask kinsmen on Satawal for a canoe or the material necessary to build one, since the latter, being a larger and higher island, has a greater reserve of timber than does the former. The scarcity of materials, construction time, and skill necessary for building a canoe makes economic transactions involving them among the most important in the Western Carolines. During the 15 months of my residence on Lamotrek three men of the island received small paddling canoes, which they had previously requested, from clan mates on Satawal. In addition a *sennap* on Satawal was building a large sailing canoe for Tagilimal, his subclan mate on Lamotrek. In two of the cases involving paddling canoes payment for each was made at the time of delivery. In the third case complete payment was deferred. If these transactions had taken place between non-kinsmen, one of the parties would most likely have shifted residence to the island of the other and payment for the work would have occurred when the craft was completed. Two of the sailing canoes in use on Lamotrek were obtained from neighboring islands in the recent past—one from Satawal and the other from Puluwat. A man of Igüfail's lineage obtained the first patrilaterally—from the lineage of his father—on Satawal. He had traveled to Satawal after the 1958 typhoon, which had destroyed his canoes on Lamotrek. He arranged the transaction on Satawal and two weeks after his return to Lamotrek he sent 30 *tur* and 50 dollars to this lineage.

The second sailing canoe, which was built on Puluwat, is the largest on the island. It, too, was obtained after the 1958 typhoon. Isïpito, a Puluwat man of Gailangùwoleai clan who has lived uxorilocally on Lamotrek for more than 30 years, obtained the craft from his brother, who still lives on that island—hence, from his own lineage. Payment was shared by Isïpito's wife's lineage—Saufalacheg—and Umai's Mòngalïfach lineage, because he also has close kin ties with Puluwat. Smaller contributions were made by all the other lineages on the island, at the request of the chiefs, since they felt that a canoe of this size would benefit the whole community and they knew that its cost was too great for one lineage to bear, especially after a typhoon. Thus, the lineages of the two prime contributors jointly own this craft, but because of the additional contributions made by all residents of the island, the canoe can be used by any lineage or navigator if the task will benefit the island as a whole. Payment for this canoe was shared as follows. Isïpito's wife's lineage contributed 20 *tur* and 500 fathoms of *holùhol*. Umai's lineage contributed 30 *tur*. And the other lineages of the island, through the chiefs, furnished 1,000 fathoms of sennit rope. No money changed hands in this transaction.

Obviously the value of a small paddling canoe is much less than

that of one of the sailing craft. For example, one of the three
mentioned above, which had been built for Urpi by his Mòngalïfach
subclan mates on Satawal, was valued at 2 gallons of kerosene,
10 small packets of tobacco, 2 *tur*, 1 piglet, 100 fathoms of *holühol*,
and 15 dollars. It is probable that the transaction involving Tagilimal's sailing canoe will be concluded in a way similar to those
above.

When a resident of Satawal makes an economic demand of a
Lamotrek kinsman, his request will not involve anything as valuable as a canoe. He will usually ask for tobacco, livestock, or
foreign trade goods (i.e., cloth, matches, sugar, etc.). Very little
tobacco is grown on Satawal—either soil or ground-water conditions seem to make for inferior yields. The scarcity of foreign
goods on this island occurs when the trading ship is occasionally
forced to bypass it because of unfavorable sea conditions and an
unsheltered anchorage. The greater proportion of goods which
flow from Lamotrek to Satawal, however, are not requested articles
but gifts which are ostensibly freely offered.

Gift Exchange

Mauss (1954) long ago pointed out the factor of reciprocity in
the exchange of gifts. Gifts (*hafang*) usually are exchanged between subunits (i.e. subclans, lineages) of clans or between groups
of individuals from different clans. Exchange on an individual

Plate 41. A canoe from Satawal preparing to depart from Lamotrek after
loading gifts.

basis is limited to formalized friendships. Often it would appear that gift exchange reciprocally balances certain Lamotrekan rights over Satawal, especially their right to request contracted exchange on a large scale. Observation of arriving Satawal canoes on Lamotrek indicated that only half bring gifts in any appreciable number for clan or subclan mates. These gifts are usually either turmeric (used as a cosmetic), steel for fishing spears, *tügakh*, food, and vinegar. The first three items are obtained by the Satawalese from atolls farther to the east or directly from Truk (where the first two originate). Vinegar is manufactured on Satawal itself—as it is on most of the islands of the Western Carolines—from fermented palm sap. A canoe departing for Satawal, on the other hand, invariably carries a fairly large number of gifts, of which tobacco is by far the most important. A single canoe may return to that island with as much as 15 or 20 pounds destined for various kin of Lamotrekans. A typical Satawal-Lamotrek exchange occurred in September, 1962. A canoe arrived from Satawal with the following gifts:

Gift	From:	To:
1 basket breadfruit	Yalùmai	Tagilimal
1 basket breadfruit	Yalùmai	Umai
1 basket taro	Igùpu	Lekaut (originally from Satawal)
1 bottle vinegar	Yalùmai	Taromai (Saufalacheg)
2 fishing spears	Yalùmai	Pakalimei (Gailangùwoleai), Taromai

When this canoe returned to Satawal, though, it carried the following:

Gift	From:	To:
50 coconuts	All lineages	Crew
50 lbs. rice	Tagilimal, Tirpo	Ekau (*tamol* of Satawal)
1 carton matches, 2 lbs. tobacco	Tagilimal, Tirpo	Ekau, Igùpu, Lukho
½ lb. tobacco	Ojaitur	Igùpu
½ lb. tobacco, 10 fishhooks	Pocheg	Igùfich
1 pig, 6 yds. cloth	Urpi	Yalùmai
2 yds. cloth	Urpi	Lukho
2 chickens	Tua (Elato)	Yachemai, Ekao
1 chicken	Tua	Yapo
1 dog	Pakairam	Eiulumel

In addition, several smaller packages of tobacco were sent to Satawal via this canoe from other Lamotrekan men, but it was not possible to record all of these transactions. It can be seen, though, that some of these gifts are returns to Satawalese who have sent gifts to Lamotrekans on this particular voyage and others are not. This is possible because an individual of one lineage who sends a gift to a subclan or clan mate on another island may or may not receive an immediate return gift. When I inquired about return gifts received for the tobacco most Lamotrekans insisted that none were expected or received. The tobacco was merely sent as an act of generosity to clansmen or friends. If, indeed, there were no reciprocity involved there would be no reasonable explanation why gifts should continue to be offered. It is probable, though, that gift exchange of this type can be viewed as part of a wider scheme of transactions and thus may be offered for one of several reasons. The most common are: (1) In anticipation of asking a favor of a kinsman on Satawal (as in arranging contractual exchange for building a canoe). (2) As a symbolic acknowledgment of a favor rendered Lamotrekans by Satawalese. The more numerous voyages the latter make to Lamotrek are one such favor, for they not only provide a means of communication between these two islands, but they also allow Lamotrek to have more frequent communication with the islands farther east. (3) As an expression of Lamotrek's political superiority over Satawal.

Gift exchange between Lamotrek and Elato occurs on a smaller scale than that between either of these islands and Satawal. In part this is because the population of Elato is quite small and the island seems to be more self-sufficient. Additionally, though, the fact that Elato and Lamotrek are islands physiographically similar means that the needs of Elato, like those of Lamotrek, can be met more easily by an island which has somewhat variable and more numerous resources. Satawal fills some of these needs. The exchange which does occur between Elato and Lamotrek usually involves food or tobacco. One example of food exchange seems typical of the interdependence relationship which exists between all three of these islands. In the early part of January, 1963, the seas in the Lamotrek-Elato area ran extremely high for several days as a storm passed to the north. The pressure of these seas on the reef forced sea water to displace part of the fresh-water lens beneath Elato Island. This salt water contaminated a portion of the taro swamp and destroyed

Plate 42. The canoe sailing from the island for home.

the taro which was growing there. This phenomenon, which is a recognized hazard to taro cultivation, is called *tatïbwül* (sea water of the swamp). A canoe was sent to Lamotrek where kin of the Elatoans who had experienced the loss were informed. As a result these Lamotrek lineage members sent a gift of ten bundles of taro (about 15 pounds each) to their clan mates on Elato. If the crop damage had covered a major portion of the Elatoan *bwül* it is quite likely that the gift offered would have been made on an island level and thus would have been a political as well as an economic and kinship transaction. Food gifts from one island to another—rather than one kin group to another—can flow in both directions between these islands. Twice during my stay on Lamotrek a canoe arrived from Elato bringing two and three live turtles to the island as gifts. The rules by which turtles are distributed, as described in Chapter 4, required that shares be given to the total population of the island rather than restricted to one particular clan or subclan. The Elatoans who brought the turtles told the chiefs of Lamotrek that there was a shortage of tobacco on their island. Thus, the chiefs directed every lineage of the island to provide the canoe with some tobacco before it returned to its home island. In addition to the live turtles these canoes also brought several baskets of cooked turtle meat to be given to specific kin groups. Cooked meat has already gone through the act of distribution on the island where it originated; thus it was possible for this meat to be sent by specific lineages on Elato directly to related lineages on Lamotrek. The Lamotrek lineage would probably reciprocate in one way or another, but most likely at a later date.

Marriage and Adoption

Whether or not one wishes to consider marriage and adoption as either "exchange of women" or "exchange of children" there are enough undeniable economic transactions between the two kin groups associated with any marriage or adoption to warrant their discussion here. Chapter 3 pointed out that the frequency of marriage for both men and women on Lamotrek is high, averaging between three and four during the lifetime of each adult. Of the marriageable adult population on Lamotrek 38 per cent had, on at least one occasion, married an individual from another island. And of these, 35 per cent were first marriages, hence arranged. The final percentage of inter-island marriages is probably higher, for complete records of Lamotrek men who have moved to other islands for this purpose were not obtained.

Obviously, one of the first requisites in an inter-island marriage is for one of the participants to change his island of residence. Since postmarital residence is usually matrilocal a man will move to the island of his wife. Nevertheless, in most cases of inter-island marriage the change in residence may not be abrupt, as the initial acquaintance of the two parties and/or their lineages will have occurred while one of the two individuals was living on the island of the other. Premarital residence on an island other than one's own may be for one or more of the following reasons.

A change of residence commonly occurs when an individual is adopted. The reasons for adoption are much the same when it occurs between kin groups of different islands as when it occurs on an intra-island level. Inter-island adoption is certainly less frequent than the former, but it is by no means rare. Three children (below 13 years of age) in 1962-63 on Lamotrek had been adopted from other islands: one each from Elato, Woleai, and Satawal. Although such children may or may not remain with their adoptive parents continually until marriage, they will retain certain rights to land on

Lamotrek. Activation of these rights will depend on residence, and if postmarital residence is established on the island of the adoptive parents the individual will retain active rights to exploit this land. Premarital residence change may also occur for reasons only indirectly related to adoption. An individual may change his residence in order to implement a claim to the land of his father. If one's father is from another island this will mean moving to that island. One may make such a claim if the father specifically gives rights to the land to his own children, but also if the child had been patrilaterally adopted, as previous statistics have shown is quite common, then he will have rights to the land in either case.

Because of the above circumstances inter-island marriage is often self-perpetuating. For example, a man of Satawal who marries a woman of Lamotrek may allow one of his children by this wife to be adopted by his own lineage. This child will either move to Satawal to be raised or he may go to that island at a later date to make a claim to the land of his father and his adoptive lineage. At such time he often will marry a woman of that island and remain there by moving to his wife's residence, but through exploitation he can continue to maintain rights to his adoptive or patrilateral land on the island. Indeed, one of his main motives for moving to the island may be to seek a wife who is unavailable on his own island. The land claim may be secondary, but a legitimate excuse for changing residence. Since adoption is arranged before the birth of the child, in at least half of the cases the adopted individual is a girl. In these cases there may be a double residence change between islands. The girl may move to her adoptive parents' island (which may be a patrilateral change), then if she marries a man of that island, she may either remain matrilocally on patrilateral land or she may move back to her true lineage land on the island of her birth and establish matrilocal residence there. In this case, too, inter-island marriage would often be self-perpetuating.

In all forms of inter-island marriage, postmarital residence is not as restricted as it is in the case of intra-island unions. A man who moves to the island of his wife almost invariably spends three or four months of each year living with his lineage on his home island, if at all possible. The self-perpetuating feature of inter-island marriage arises here because the children of this man will often accompany their parents during these residence changes. As a result, they are more likely to make a claim to their father's land sometime in

the future, either because the father specifically gives them rights
to it or simply by virtue of the precedence that has been established by past residence on it.

Inter-island marriage, residence change, and land claims may
reach from the Lamotrek-Elato area to islands as far away as
Puluwat and Pulusuk. One man of Lamotrek who was adopted
to Puluwat spent much of his youth there and married a Puluwat
woman. He later returned to Lamotrek and again married. One of
his daughters by this latter marriage moved to Puluwat, where she
now lives on her father's adoptive land. This was possible because
there was no longer anyone on Puluwat who had more direct rights
to it. A son of this Lamotrek man has joined his sister on Puluwat,
where he now lives and helps work the land. The girl has married
a Puluwat man. The brother has not yet married, but there is every
reason to expect him to in the near future.

A final common reason for changing islands of residence occurs
when an individual leaves his own lineage land and goes to another
island to live with a branch of his own clan or subclan. The moti-
vation for such a move may specifically be to find a wife, since
there may be no woman available on his own island who is acceptable to the individual or his lineage. Such circumstances are not
uncommon. A population of only 200 individuals, at any one time,
often has a large disparity between the number of marriageable
males and females. In 1962, for example, there were five or six young
men nearing marriageable age on Lamotrek, whereas only two girls
were then available. Two of the men were restricted in their choice
because they were related to one or the other of these girls. Thus,
they had the choice of either waiting for another girl to reach
marriageable age or they could seek a wife on another island. In the
case of two of these young men the move was quite likely, for both
had ties to other islands. The father of one had come from Woleai
and thus by virtue of patrilateral rights he left for that island early
in 1963 to reside with his father's lineage. Although marriage was
not mentioned as a specific reason for this move, it is quite likely
that he will marry before he returns. In the case of the second of
these men his mother was from Faraulep and had moved to Lamotrek because of an old land claim of her lineage. It is likely that
he will return to Faraulep if he does not soon choose a wife on
Lamotrek. An individual may change residence to another island
to live with his subclan or clan mates for several other reasons, land

claims being foremost among them. The case involving Puluwat which was cited above is such an example. Such a move often happens as a result of depopulation, where subclans and clans have become extinct on more than one island. It is a means of retaining land in a subclan and not permitting alternate means of inheritance to alienate the land to another subclan or clan.

ECONOMIC AND POLITICAL TIES

Inter-island ties of economic and political significance involve larger groups and function at a more complex level of organization than do the ties described in the preceding section. In the pre-contact and early contact periods of which Lessa (1950) speaks, the Yapese network was the broadest politicoeconomic organizational system among the Western Carolines, but most of these ties with Yap have long since been severed. Nevertheless, the ties which bound the outer islands to Yap function between smaller groupings of these islands which were formerly components of the larger system. The basis for these ties is the same in either case and the circumstances which give rise to them still prevail. Thus, although certain of the symbolic features of inter-island politicoeconomic organization between Lamotrek, Elato, and Satawal were abandoned in 1953 (as a result of missionary influence), these underlying ties still govern most present-day inter-island political behavior between these three islands.

The *Hù*

The Lamotrek-Elato-Satawal inter-island organization was called the *Hù* (fishhook). According to this system Lamotrek was politically status ranked above Satawal and Elato. And economically, the latter two islands were required to send semiannual tribute to Lamotrek.

The people of the Western Carolines divide the year into two seasons. The distinction between these seasons is based on a change in prevailing winds and the bearing season of breadfruit trees. Once each season the Satawalese and Elatoans were obligated to send tribute to Lamotrek. The Satawal chief—sometime during the breadfruit season—would require each *bwogat* on his island to contribute one basket of preserved breadfruit (*mar*) as its share of the tribute payment, and the total (which averaged 15 baskets of

25 pounds each) would be taken to Lamotrek. During the following season the Satawal chief would similarly assemble 1,000 ripe coconuts (*sho*) as tribute. Five sailing canoes were needed to transport each of these tribute payments to the paramount chief at Lamïtakh on Lamotrek. The Lamotrek *tamolüfalu* would distribute the *mar* or *sho* to all *bwogat* of the island according to the regular pattern of allotment. Similarly, once each season the resident chief of Elato would send three live turtles to Lamotrek as his island's tribute. There was no seasonal variation in the type of tribute extracted from this island.

Lamotrek, on an island level, was not required to send anything to either Satawal or Elato in return for tribute received. However, if a surplus of fish were available they might choose to do so. Knowing the usual patterns of exchange, it was inevitable, though, that these visiting canoes would leave Lamotrek with large amounts of tobacco and other gifts destined for specific lineages and subclan members on the respective islands, but this individual and kin group level of exchange could not be considered reciprocal in either quality or quantity for island-level tribute. Reciprocity for the "right" of Lamotrek to demand and receive tribute from Satawal and Elato was in the form of other "rights" granted to these islands by Lamotrek.

Satawal-Elato Exploitation Rights

In times of natural disaster individual lineages, subclans, or clans can turn to co-members on other islands for assistance. The *tatïbwül* discussed above showed how this occurs. If the disaster is severe it is also possible, because of the inter-island political organization, to ask for assistance on an island level and not via kin groups. Yapoig, the paramount chief (Mòngalïfach) of Satawal, made such a request after the 1958 typhoon. He asked Lefaioup, the Lamotrek paramount chief, for several canoe loads of ripe coconuts. Although Lamotrek had also been severely damaged by the storm, Lefaioup readily agreed to furnish the nuts and she continued to do so at intervals through 1960. Lamotrek would also have had the right to ask for similar assistance from either Satawal or Elato, but one could easily have justified this on the basis of the former island's superior status ranking. But in any case, it is apparent that the politico-economic organization of the *Hü* permits islands of lower status to make such a request and does not allow Lamotrek to refuse it. In part, the tribute payments maintain this system.

There is also an important and continuous right of exploitation granted Elato and Satawal by Lamotrek. This is the right of exploitation on nearby uninhabited islands, reefs, and lagoons. Olimarao, Lamaliur, Pikh, and Pikhailo are all under the eminent domain of the paramount chief of Lamotrek. None of these atolls or islands is divided into clan-held plots as are the uninhabited islands of Lamotrek Atoll itself. With few exceptions use rights to the products of these uninhabited islands are granted to all inhabitants of Lamotrek, Elato, and Satawal for normal exploitation of their subsistence resources. The right of eminent domain was a fundamental concept of the whole Yapese network. This point was made clear by several informants on Yap whom I questioned before arriving on Lamotrek. One of these Yapese said he was not too concerned that the outer islanders had stopped sending tribute to the Yapese, but he was upset over the fact that the outer island land was no longer under their control. A second informant stated that during German times the outer islanders had to provide the trader O'Keefe with copra as partial payment for the transporting of stone-money from Palau to Yap. It was also during these years that a percentage of the money received from the Germans for leased land on the outer islands was forwarded by these islanders to the Yapese. More recently, several Yapese were said to be upset by the fact that when Ulithi leased Falalap Island to the U.S. Coast Guard, in order that a Loran station could be built there, these islanders did not send a portion of these funds to the relevant *sawei* partners on Yap. One rumor which was current on Yap at that time held that Yapese magicians had been responsible for both the recent typhoon which had struck Ulithi and the lightning which had hit a canoe of this island. The magicians had taken these measures because Ulithi refused to recognize the right of eminent domain in the Falalap transaction.

Returning to those islands of direct concern here, though, the importance of the four outlying uninhabited islands to the people of Satawal and Elato was mentioned in Chapter 2. Satawal relies heavily on Pikhailo and to a lesser degree on Pikh for a large percentage of her yearly sea turtle catch as well as the numerous reef fish taken at this atoll. Canoe travel between Pikhailo and Satawal is nearly continuous during favorable weather. Thus, turtles and fish caught there are quickly taken to Satawal for distribution. Pikh is less often exploited by the Satawalese both because it is more distant and because it is a less fruitful area. Pikh, like Satawal, is a raised coral island with no lagoon. The only advantage it has over Satawal as a resource area is that, as an uninhabited island, its marine resources are more abundant because of infrequent exploitation. Since the population of Elato is small, while its resource areas are comparatively large, the people here are less dependent than the Satawalese on neighboring islands and reefs for subsistence products. Elato canoes do not often visit Olimarao. Exploitation of nearby Lamaliur, though, is frequent. Lamaliur is the prime turtle-hunting ground for the Elatoans as well as the Lamotrekans.

Puluwat and Pulusuk are the only other islands which exploit Pikh or Pikhailo with any frequency. And usually canoes from these two islands only stop at Pikh and Pikhailo on voyages to Satawal and/or Lamotrek. Thus, their primary purpose is not exploitation, but merely replenishment of stores. Nevertheless, it should be recalled that at one time Puluwat and Pulusuk were also involved in the tribute system.

I have no evidence that islands west of Elato ever exploited with any regularity the outlying islands claimed by Lamotrek. Faraulep had closer and more productive turtle grounds at Gaferut, while Woleai and Ifaluk are more distant. And of the three, only Ifalukans seem to have a real need for additional resource areas as evidenced by their trips to the submerged reefs north of their island (Burrows and Spiro 1953:120).

A symbolic act directly related to the recognition of Lamotrek's suzerainty over the outlying islands mentioned is carried out by individuals of Elato, Satawal, Puluwat, and Pulusuk whenever they meet Lamotrekans on one of the uninhabited islands. These islanders must give the Lamotrekans at least one head from any turtles taken on these islands. One will remember that the heads of turtles taken on Lamotrek are offered to the paramount chief during distribution. In summary, it is apparent that those islands of lower status which pay tribute to Lamotrek are those islands which exploit resource areas belonging to Lamotrek. Changes in this system which have been stimulated by foreign administrative and commercial activities have not altered its fundamental organization. A brief outline of foreign influence in the Carolines was given in Chapter 1. More detailed comments are now in order for the Lamotrek-Elato-Satawal area.

Foreign Administrations and Trade

Although Wilson sighted Satawal and Lamotrek in 1797, outside commerce with these islands was infrequent until 1880, when the English copra trader Lewis settled on Lamotrek (Krämer 1937:9). The navigational ability of the islanders, though, had permitted foreign manufactured goods to enter these islands indirectly before 1797. The German government was primarily interested in the Western Carolines as an area of commercial exploitation. In fact German traders had been active in the area long before the government purchased the island from Spain (Tetens 1958:47 ff.). Kaneshiro (1950:2) reports that the trading firm of Mischgott and Pomarett purchased Pugue and Falaite from the Lamotrekans, but the details of this transaction are not remembered. The Japanese administration of the Carolines, following World War I, resulted in increased commercial exploitation—including recruited and forced labor—primary schooling for outer island children, and military fortifications on many of the outer islands (including Lamotrek). During these years, all of the young men who were physically able spent one or more years working for the Japanese on Fais, Palau, or Yap. Several of the young boys of this same period went to the primary school on Yap. Japanese commercial exploitation of the islands followed a pattern similar to that of the Germans. The government and trading company expropriated the uninhabited islands and, in the case of Satawal, large tracts of land on the windward side of the island. Copra was the most important exportable crop and the local residents were employed by the trading company to exploit this product on these lands (Kaneshiro 1950:2). Any additional copra which was produced from their own land holdings was also bought by the trading company.[1] The Japanese administration forbade long-distance canoe travel in the Western Carolines, ostensibly because the canoes often got lost. This prohibition and the fact that many men were working away from their home islands did much to decrease the frequency of tribute payments to Yap, although such were occasionally sent via the trading ship. The travel

---

[1] The records of copra exports during the years of Japanese administration were destroyed during the war (Iwasaki, personal communication, Statistics Bureau of the Prime Minister's Office).

prohibition among the outer islands was not too effective, though, and canoe traffic between smaller groups of islands such as Lamotrek, Elato, and Satawal did not decrease appreciably. In the mid-1930's a meteorological observation station was established by the Japanese on Lamotrek and several years later a seaplane base. This base was destroyed during the war, but the island itself was little damaged and no local residents were killed or injured. At the end of the war a total of 25 Japanese were stationed on Lamotrek (Richard 1957(2):20). During this same period there were no Japanese on Elato and only three traders living on Satawal. None of the military personnel openly took local women as wives, but several of the civilian employees did. Today there are four men and two women on Lamotrek who are offspring of such marriages. One man on Satawal had a Japanese father. No one on Elato, however, seems to be the result of such a union.

The frequency of contact between the outer islands and foreigners has not increased since the United States took over administration of the area in 1945; the administration trading ship visits the islands three or four times a year. All of the land expropriated by the Japanese has been returned to the islanders and has been redistributed to the original clan owners. Although the precise boundary lines were no longer remembered, new divisions were agreed to by the parties concerned. Those uninhabited islands which were not subdivided into individually owned plots (i.e., Olimarao, Lamaliur, Pikhailo, Pikh) are again recognized as belonging to Lamotrek and her paramount chief. The expropriation and redistribution of land during German, Japanese, and American periods of control has not disrupted in any fundamental way the traditional patterns of exploitation on these public lands, primarily because of the distinction between subsistence and commercial exploitation. Turtle hunting on the uninhabited islands was carried on much as before by those workers employed by the trading company to make copra there. And the copra itself was not necessary for survival.

Today, copra produced by the outer islanders is sold to the Yap Trading Company, which is a cooperative primarily controlled by the inhabitants of that island. The price paid for copra is stabilized and occasionally subsidized by the government at four cents per pound. In 1950 Lamotrek sold a little more than $2,000 worth of copra and purchased nearly $1,700 worth of trade goods. Expenditures for fishing equipment, tobacco, matches, knives, cloth, and dyes were of greater importance than those for food (Kaneshiro 1950:3). The $300 surplus which was not spent on trade goods was either saved or spent by outer island students and visitors while on Yap or Palau. After the typhoon of 1958 copra sales stopped on Lamotrek and purchases from savings were very small. The administration supplied supplementary food—rice, flour, powdered milk, and sugar—for a year until agricultural production was sufficient to support the population. Some Yapese claimed that it was just this practice, which started in German times, that has led to the breakdown of the *sawei* system, i.e., if the outer islanders can depend on the foreign administration for surplus foods during times of shortages, then they need not approach the Yapese for similar help. Copra sales on Lamotrek did not resume for over three years. At the time of my arrival such sales were just resuming. In August of 1962, for example, about $500 worth of copra was sold on Lamotrek, and the purchases from the trading ship were as follows:

Goods	Amount		Price
Food			
Sardines	5 cases		$50.40
Ship biscuits	4 cases		50.20
Rice	250 lbs.		31.25
Sugar	100 lbs.		14.88
Shoyu	2 btls.		1.90
		Subtotal	$148.63
Clothing			
Cloth	4 bolts		73.80
Sandals	6 pairs		3.30
		Subtotal	77.10
Fishing Equipment			
Rubber tubing	2 rolls		22.50
Flashlights	4		4.20
Batteries	2 doz.		3.75
		Subtotal	30.45
Miscellaneous			
Kerosene	55 gals.		38.50
Matches	1 case		18.00
Cigarettes	25 cartons		52.50
Soap	1 case		5.40
		Subtotal	114.40
		Total	$370.58

In this particular case 40 per cent of the purchases were for food items, which invariably would be consumed on special occasions, e.g., funeral feasts, saints' days, celebrations, etc. Copra sales by 1963 were much larger per voyage, but the total yearly sales were still below the 1950 level. Purchases were still largely restricted to necessities, as the above, and as the total expenditures increased the percentage spent on food decreased. As far as basic subsistence is concerned the Lamotrekans, Elatoans, and Satawalese could survive without making any purchases from the trading company. And even the manufactured goods which are bought could be produced in inferior quality from local products or obtained in trade from voyages made to Truk by canoe. The commercial value of coconuts, though, has resulted in more intensive cultivation of them. As a food, coconuts are used for drinking and as a condiment with taro and breadfruit. On Lamotrek, Elato, and Satawal they are seldom eaten as a staple. Nevertheless, because of their commercial value areas of the islands which were once undergrowth or covered with nonproductive trees have been cleared and replanted in this crop.

Commercial Exploitation and Modern Tribute

Satawal and Elato stopped sending traditional semiannual tribute payments to Lamotrek in 1953. My informants on Lamotrek claim that they abandoned the tribute because of conversion to Christianity. Nevertheless, turtle heads continue to be presented as before and, in addition, tribute payments of a more modern type are now made, which function as did the old: to symbolize Lamotrek's right of eminent domain over outlying islands and her superior status ranking. Although the paramount chief of Lamotrek now permits the inhabitants of any neighboring island to exploit the subsistence resources of the uninhabited islands while rejecting their tribute, she has not made any such concession to the Satawalese and Elatoans as far as commercial exploitation of these same islands is concerned.

Copra is the only commercially valuable product taken from the outlying islands. Olimarao and Lamaliur have large reserves of palms, but the coconut output of Pikhailo and Pikh is too small to be of value. As pointed out earlier, Lamotrekans and Elatoans travel to Olimarao and Lamaliur for copra production at least as often as they do for subsistence exploitation. Income which is derived from copra sales is held by the lineage of the producer. For this reason, restrictions have been placed on the commercial use of communally held trees by the chiefs of Lamotrek and are enforced by the paramount chief. Thus, any group of individuals which plans to go either to Lamaliur or Olimarao for the purpose of making copra must first obtain permission from the paramount chief to do so. If the individuals involved are Elatoans and the paramount chief is resident on Lamotrek, then they must first voyage to Lamotrek before proceeding to Lamaliur or Olimarao. Every sack of copra produced on Olimarao or Lamaliur is taxed 50 cents by the chief and this money is turned over to her. She will use it to purchase goods for the benefit of the community, but she can also spend it on segments of the population as she sees fit. This copra tax can be likened to a tribute payment. Satawalese do not pay it, for they make no copra on Pikh or Pikhailo; the Elatoans do, though, when they exploit Lamaliur or Olimarao. Although Falaite and Pugue are also valuable copra areas· no tax is paid on the produce of these islands, for they are subdivided into lineage-held plots.

The right of eminent domain over Olimarao and Lamaliur is rigorously guarded. Early in 1963, while the paramount chief of Lamotrek was resident on Elato, two men (one of whom was a resident of Elato) set out from Lamotrek to make copra on Lamaliur. They did not stop at Elato to obtain permission from the paramount chief. No one was making copra on Olimarao or Pugue at this time but several men were doing so on their lineage holdings on Falaite. Shortly after the two men returned from Lamaliur with ten sacks of copra, the paramount chief returned from Elato. She heard of the copra-making activities and became quite angry. She fined the men who had worked Lamaliur 50 cents per sack; thus, their total debt to her was one dollar per sack on copra which was selling for about four dollars. Lefaioup then refused to allow anyone to make copra on Olimarao for three months because of the above violation and the fact that large areas of lineage-owned land on Pugue remained unexploited. This prohibition covered the last three months of my stay on Lamotrek and during this time no one attempted to travel there for the purpose of copra production, few people voiced open dissatisfaction with the ruling, and all admitted—either eagerly or reluctantly, depending on their position in the dispute—the right of the *tamolúfalu* to make such a ruling. Before 1953 failure to forward tribute payments to Lamotrek could have resulted in a similar prohibition on the use of the outlying islands as subsistence areas.

In summary, then, exploitation of copra as a cash crop has not altered the fundamental patterns of subsistence and exchange. The copra sold is a surplus which would not be utilized by the islanders as food. And when it is necessary to make a choice between having enough copra to eat and enough to sell—as in the recovery period following a typhoon—none will be sold. The production of copra has not necessitated a basic change in traditional agricultural patterns. Coconut trees are a subsistence crop with traditional techniques of cultivation. The Western Carolines have been able to adjust to a world economy without having to begin cultivation of new cash crops with unfamiliar requirements which might have necessitated the development of new patterns of land tenure. The distribution of purchased trade goods has also followed traditional patterns. The majority of goods purchased are substitutions for locally produced necessities. Today one might spend his time making copra in order to buy sail canvas or broadcloth instead of manufacturing these items from locally available materials. And since men would be the workers in either case, the change to copra production has not necessitated a change in the division of labor.

POLITICAL AND KIN TIES

Since clans and subclans are not localized on a single island and intermarriage between islands is a frequent occurrence, kinship ties between islands are extensive. This has relevance in the political, as well as economic, sphere of organization. Clans and their composite units (subclans, lineages, and descent lines) are ranked within the social organization of a single island. And islands themselves are similarly ranked with respect to each other. In those cases of inter-island political activity cited above, it was shown that chiefs dealt with chiefs regardless of how their respective clans would be ranked on each other's island. For example, the paramount chief of Lamotrek, who is of Mòngalïfach clan, would deal directly with the paramount chief of Woleai, who is Gailangùwoleai, a clan ranked quite low on Lamotrek. Nevertheless, since inter-island affairs are carried out on a different level of social organization than intra-island and kin group affairs, it is the rank of the island as a whole, and not that of its constituent clans, that is important. Kin groups on different islands can deal with one another as they would on a single island, but such interaction would not concern the total population of either island. Examples of interaction between subclans of Elato, Satawal, and Lamotrek will show, though, that the respective subclan divisions are ranked according to the general ranking of the island on which they are found.

Chiefly Clans and Island-Level Organization

The ranking of the chiefs of Lamotrek was discussed in Chapter 3. The political organization of Elato and Satawal is similar to that already discussed for Lamotrek. On Elato there are two chiefly clans, Móngalïfach and Saufalacheg, and three nonchiefly, Gailangü-woleai, Sauwel, and Hofalu. Satawal has three chiefs, two of whom are drawn from Móngalïfach and one from Hatoliar. The nonchiefly clans on this island are Hatamang, Saosatawal, Sauwel, Hofalu,[2] and Masùlug. All three of these islands, then, have an odd number of land-holding clans—seven each on Lamotrek and Satawal and five on Elato. The residence patterns and land tenure on Satawal and Elato support the triadic/dualistic divisions discussed with respect to Lamotrek.

On Elato the paramount chief is the same individual who holds this rank on Lamotrek, while the chief of Saufalacheg is the senior member of a specific subclan on the island; he is not the same Saufalacheg chief as is found on Lamotrek. The proximity of Lamotrek to Elato presumably made it possible for the paramount chief of the former to maintain close control over the latter, since the particular clan concerned was of highest rank on both. Nevertheless, day-to-day activities require decisions made by a resident chief and the Saufalacheg *tamol* acts in this capacity. When resident on Elato the paramount chief stayed at Latao in the southern district.[3] The Saufalacheg *tamol* came from the middle of the island and while there was no third chief, *ochang*, who were Sauwel on this island, came from the north. There were two men's houses on Elato, but both have been abandoned, as has the one on Lamotrek. Their ruins still stand on the island (Map 12); one was for the use of men from chiefly clans and the other for men of nonchiefly clan status. They were found, as would be expected, on land controlled respectively by chiefly and nonchiefly clans. Today the subclan of Saufalacheg from which the *tamol* was chosen has expired on the island. Le-

---

[2] On Satawal Hofalu *hailang* is also called Pikh *hailang*.

[3] Maps 12 and 13 are labeled according to the original land-holding clans. Several of the *bwogat* have changed hands in recent years for the same reasons that other *bwogat* have changed ownership on Lamotrek.

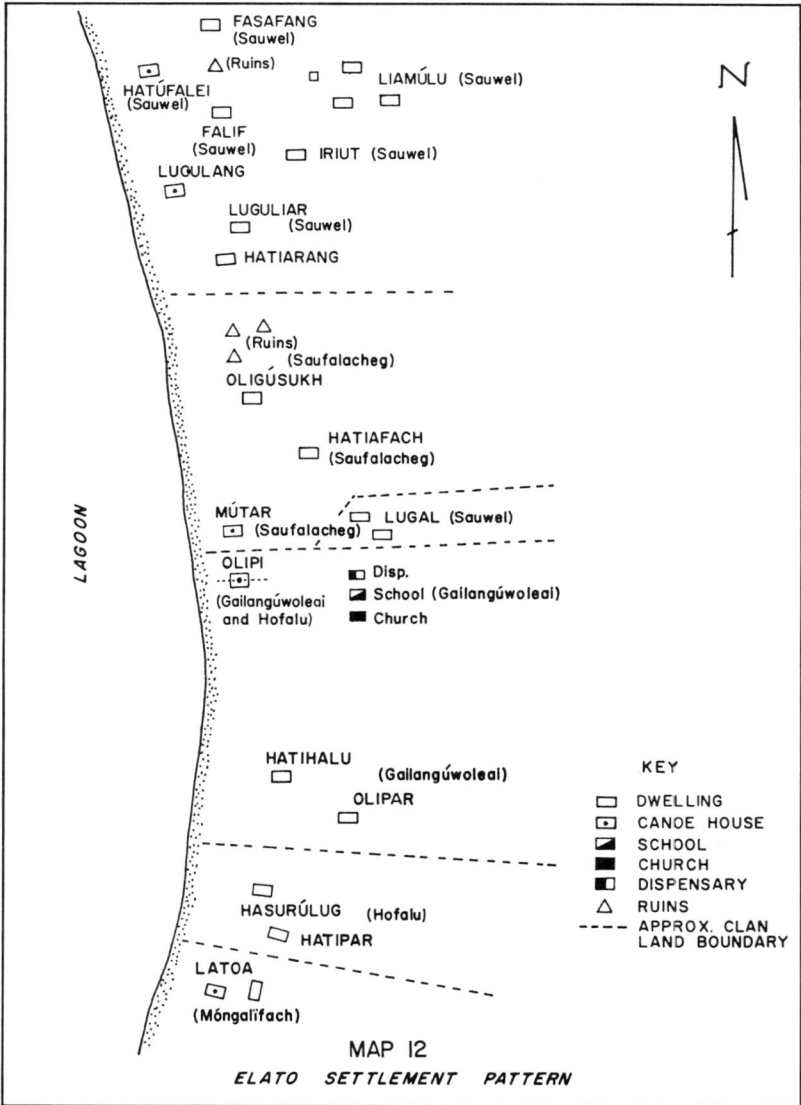

MAP 12
ELATO SETTLEMENT PATTERN

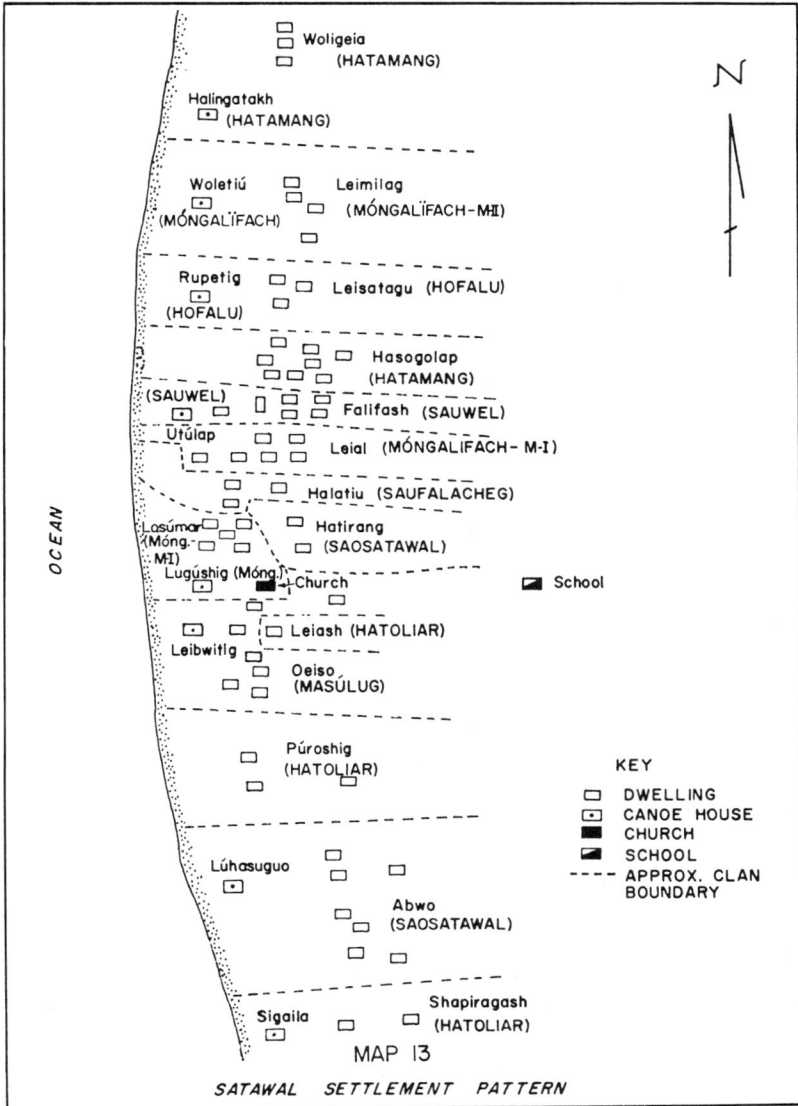

Woligeia
(HATAMANG)

Halingatakh
(HATAMANG)

N

Woletiú   Leimilag
(MÓNGALÏFACH)   (MÓNGALÏFACH-M-II)

Rupetig   Leisatagu (HOFALU)
(HOFALU)

Hasogolap
(HATAMANG)

(SAUWEL)
                 Falifash (SAUWEL)
Utúlap   Leial (MÓNGALÏFACH- M-I)

Halatiu (SAUFALACHEG)

Lasúmar   Hatirang
(Móng.   (SAOSATAWAL)
M-I)
Lugúshig (Móng.)
                 Church   School

                 Leiash (HATOLIAR)
Leibwitig

                 Oeiso
                 (MASÚLUG)

Púroshig
(HATOLIAR)

                                     KEY
                                     ☐ DWELLING
                                     ⊡ CANOE HOUSE
                                     ■ CHURCH
Lúhasuguo   ◨ SCHOOL
                                     ---- APPROX. CLAN
                 Abwo   BOUNDARY
                 (SAOSATAWAL)

Sigaila   Shapiragash
                 (HATOLIAR)

OCEAN

MAP 13

SATAWAL   SETTLEMENT   PATTERN

faioup, the *tamolùfalu*, has, therefore, appointed Malumai, a Sauwel (*ochang*) man, as acting chief. This has necessitated appointing the senior Gailangùwoleai man to a position similar to *ochang*. He is called *chalugùtug*, although his duties are those of an *ochang* member.

The three chiefs of Satawal are drawn from Mòngalïfach and Hatoliar clans. Hatamang clan is present on the island, but is not considered to be of high status. The paramount chief and third-ranking *tamol* both come from Mòngalïfach clan, but from different subclans. Yapoig, the paramount chief, is of the same subclan as Lefaioup, the *tamolùfalu* of Lamotrek. The third-ranking chief is from the same subclan (M-II) as Tagilimal and Umai. The clan of the second-ranking chief is not found on either Lamotrek or Elato. The *bwogat* of the two Satawal Mòngalïfach chiefs were north of the island's center (Map 13). Yapoig (M-I) came from Leial and Iguot (M-II) from Losùmar. The Hatoliar chief, Ekao, has his lineage seat at Leiash. By virtue of actual residence, though, the island is governed somewhat differently. Iguot controls the north, Yapoig the middle, and Ekao (who resides at Shapiragash) the south. Satawal, unlike Lamotrek and Elato, is said to have never had a men's house.

Clans, Marriage, and the Emergence of New Units

In the pre-contact past, marriage was in part dependent on the status ranking of the clans of the potential mates. For this reason kin ties between clans were more predictable than they are today. Since a chiefly clan member could only marry an individual from another chiefly clan, individuals of this status on Lamotrek were forced to choose a spouse from Mòngalïfach, Saufalacheg, or Hatamang clans. Residents of Elato were similarly restricted in choice to Mòngalïfach and Saufalacheg *hailang*, while Satawalese chiefly clan members could seek mates only from Mòngalïfach or Hatoliar. An individual from any of the above clans, though, could marry into a chiefly clan of another island regardless of the status of that clan on his own island. This restrictive rule seems to have encouraged two developments. First, there was an increase in the number of inter-island marriages contracted. If a chiefly clan member sought a spouse from another island he not only had a larger total population within which a choice could be made, but he also had a greater number of clans into which he was permitted to marry. And second, this restrictive rule encouraged subclans within a clan to emphasize their independence—one from the other —so that eventually intermarriage between these units was permitted. I have already pointed out instances of intra-Mòngalïfach marriage on Lamotrek and I have recorded similar cases of intermarriage between individuals of Iguot's and Yapoig's subclans on Satawal. If the discrete characteristics of subclans continue to be emphasized through several generations it is possible that one will emerge as an independent clan. During the previous discussion of *bwogat* and lineages it was pointed out that kin groups are often referred to by the name of the homestead upon which they are settled, and, indeed, in the case of lineages and subclans they have no other proper name. The significance of the factor of residence as it influences kin group affiliation was also emphasized in the discussion of subclan M-IV and Hatamang on Lamotrek. Two similar trends were also noted on Satawal.

Informants on Satawal first told me that the third-ranking chief of that island came from Losùmar clan. A subsequent survey of the *bwogat* on the island revealed, though, that Losùmar was the name of a homestead and not of a *hailang*. When I again questioned my informants about this they stated that the resident lineage of Losùmar was Mòngalïfach and that properly it was only the homestead which went under this name, but in practice the lineage itself was called Losùmar to avoid confusing these individuals with those of Yapoig's subclan, which was the more senior Mòngalïfach kin group. In another case, Ekao, the second-ranking *tamol*, was said to belong to Leiash clan. But again this was not the name of the clan, but rather the name of the *bwogat* seat or *erao* of the *hailang*, even though at that time there was no one of Hatoliar affiliation living at Leiash.

In the case of Losùmar one cannot say that the sole reason for the individuals of this subclan assuming the name of the homestead in lieu of their true clan name was an attempt either at breaking away from the clan as a whole or a means to cover up the fact that intermarriage had occurred between the members of this subclan and individuals from other Mòngalïfach subclans, for, as the second case shows, the tendency for a clan to be called by its homestead's name is a common occurrence. Nevertheless, restrictive rules in clan intermarriage are probably a contributing factor which encourages adoption of the name of the *bwogat* as a substitute for

the true clan designation. In this way, at least, it is clear in everyone's mind that kin ties are not considered close. Under these conditions it is conceivable that eventually one of the subclans will
emerge as a new clan under the new name.

Clans, Islands, and Political Authority

All of the clans and subclans of Satawal view their counterparts
on Lamotrek as being of higher rank because that island, as a
whole, is ranked higher than their own. Thus Yapoig, the paramount chief of Satawal, not only must consult Lefaioup on island-
level decisions, but he must also consider her opinion on clan-level
affairs. Similarly, Iguot, the third-ranking chief of Satawal (who
is Mòngalïfach), has his counterpart in Umai, a subclan mate on
Lamotrek. Even though Umai is not a chief on Lamotrek he out-
ranks Iguot, who is a chief, because both are members of the
same subclan, and the branch of this subclan on Lamotrek is considered to be of higher status because the island itself is of higher
rank than Satawal. A recent decision made by Umai serves well to
illustrate his position vis-à-vis Iguot. Since conversion to Christianity most Lamotrekans have solidified their marriages by going
through a church ceremony. A young man of Umai's lineage who
had married a Hatamang girl in this manner decided, after two
years, to divorce her in the traditional way and take a new wife
from another lineage. Umai, though, refused to permit this since
he knew the priest would disapprove of the divorce; moreover,
the new girl was patrilaterally related to Umai and his lineage.
The young man and the girl persisted, though, and took up residence with each other. Umai and the senior man of the girl's
lineage then told the couple that they must either part or both
lineages would refuse them food from their land holdings. The
couple did not reply to this ultimatum, but instead fled to Satawal
on the first available canoe. When they arrived there Iguot, who
was a subclan mate of the young man, offered them food and
housing. Umai learned of this within a few weeks and asked Iguot
to cease giving the couple aid. Iguot, at least openly, agreed to
do as Umai suggested. The couple did not return to Lamotrek,
however, but instead moved on to the land of the adoptive parents of the girl (both the young man and the girl had been adopted
by Satawalese and had previously lived on the island for varying

lengths of time). In this way the couple moved beyond the jurisdiction of either Umai or Iguot, whose influence, in this case, is
limited to clan affairs.

The importance of intra-island clan, subclan, and lineage ranking and inter-island kin ties as they influence decision-making are
illustrated by the circumstances which lead to the choice of a
new paramount chief. If there is no clear line of inheritance to
this chieftainship on the island, succession is not a simple matter
to determine, for the clear line of inheritance stops at the boundary
between subclans. Lefaioup assumed the paramount chieftainship
of Lamotrek as the sole surviving member of her lineage and subclan. The man who was paramount chief before her came from a
different lineage of the same subclan centered at Falihoal *bwogat*,
but that line too is now extinct. Assuming that Lefaioup leaves no
heirs—which is most probable—there will be no individuals left
on the island who belong to any of the lineages of the *tamolüfalu*
subclan. Because of these circumstances, some informants felt that
succession should be by the senior man of the Möngalïfach lineage
of next highest rank on the island. It should be emphasized, though,
that most of these informants either came from one of these lineages
or from one of the nonchiefly clans on Lamotrek. Informants on
Elato and Satawal, however, felt that succession to the position of
tamolüfalu should remain within its legitimate subclan. Thus, they
said, if there were no living members of the subclan on Lamotrek
then the Lamotrekans should seek a proper subclan member from
one of the neighboring islands—preferably Satawal, since M-I is
also extinct on Elato. This latter position would seem to be the
more traditional. A similar situation is said to have occurred on
Ifaluk a few years ago, when the subclan of one of the *tamol* expired. At that time several Ifaluk men of senior standing came to
Lamotrek and asked Umai, who was of the same subclan, if he
would not come to Ifaluk and assume the chieftainship. Umai,
though, declined because of his family and property obligations
on Lamotrek. And, as previously mentioned, the Saufalacheg chieftainship of Elato is presently unoccupied. When I asked an informant why a certain Saufalacheg man on that island was not
chief, he replied that this individual was not of the proper subclan and that if a chief of Saufalacheg were installed he would have
to be sought on Woleai, for it is only there that the proper subclan still survives.

Plate 43. Men from Satawal visiting Lamotrek are shown making rope at Kulong canoe house.

Inter-Island Politics and Foreign Rule

The appearance of foreign powers in the Western Carolines has necessitated consideration of policies imposed or suggested by these authorities during the process of decision-making on individual islands. For the most part the presence of these foreign powers has not disrupted local organization to any great extent. Instead, the political adjustment which has resulted because of the new circumstances is more accurately described as an integration of such conditions into the framework of the old organization.

During the German period of administration (1899-1914), contact between outer islanders and administrators reached such frequency as to require the creation of formalized channels of communication and interaction. The *tamolnïpüsash* (chief for the "foreigner") system filled this need.[4] Accordingly, the administrator who visits Lamotrek, Elato, or Satawal meets with this individual rather than the paramount chief. The *tamolnïpüsash* is not permitted to reach final agreement with an administrator without first consulting the other chiefs of the island, particularly the paramount chief. And even these chiefs will usually delay action until they have had an opportunity to find out how the chiefs of islands of higher status regard the policy in question. On Lamotrek it is usual for the paramount chief to inform both Elato and Satawal beforehand of any policies she will have the *tamolnïpüsash* discuss with the administrator. Thus, the three islands will usually present a united front to this government representative. And conversely, if the chief of either Elato or Satawal wishes to broach a topic with the administration, he will usually inform the *tamolüfalu* of Lamotrek and assess her attitude about it. There are probably multiple reasons for the origin of this system. Basically, though, it seems to be a method of integrating a new level of political interaction into a political organization which was already dealing with inter-island problems via specific channels of communication. The position of the *tamolnïpüsash* allows outside directives to be guided into these channels and forestalls decisions on such suggestions and directives until consultation is held with islands and/ or clans of the proper status.

The individual who acts as *tamolnïpüsash* on Lamotrek is traditionally the chief of Saufalacheg, who is the second-ranking *tamol* in the island's district system. The choice of the head of Lugulap district as "chief for the foreigner" seems to have added significance when one recalls the political organization of the island. This individual would seem to function not only as a mediator between

---

[4] Krämer (1937:675) has recorded the word as *apisas* and he translates it as "European."

north and south on an island level of organization, but he would also seem to act as a buffer between the island and the administration on this supra-island level. The choice of this man, then, as *tamolnïpïusash* seems to integrate clearly the old organization with the requirements of new circumstances. Similar statements could be made about the Sauwel man on Elato who acts as *tamolnïpïusash*. The information I have on this role on Satawal is not clear so I am not able to say if the situation there is similar or different from the above.

The added authority which the *tamolnïpïusash* derives from this role—as one who deals directly with administrators—has, in some cases, resulted in a status conflict with respect to his island-level rank and the rank he assumes in supra-island affairs. On Lamotrek the *tamolnïpïusash* has occasionally attempted to increase his authority in the area of domestic and ordinary inter-island politics, an area in which he would normally have no more authority than any other clan or district chief. This has only been possible because the present paramount chief is a woman, as well as the sole surviving member of her subclan, and because the acting paramount chief is from a lesser Mòngalïfach lineage. The latter, for example, is often reluctant to exert his authority because of the tenuousness of his position with respect to other Mòngalïfach lineages, especially M-2. This power grab of the Saufalacheg chief has resulted in a great deal of friction between the various lineages of high status on Lamotrek. And occasionally these disputes are aired in matters of land ownership and decision-making. In part these arguments over minor matters have encouraged Lefaioup to spend most of her time on Elato, where she is able to avoid involvement and thus test her authority only in matters of major importance. Thus far decisions she has made have not been disputed and I doubt that they will be. For even though Saufalacheg, on many occasions, is able to play off the intra-Mòngalïfach diffusion of power to its own advantage, on any major decision the Mòngalïfach lineages would almost invariably show a united front and would be supported by the majority—if not all—of the non-chiefly clans as well as by tradition and the inter-island political organization. The play for more power on the part of Saufalacheg will probably not outlive the present chief of that clan, and he will almost certainly not survive the younger paramount chief.

On Satawal the ability of the *tamolnïpïusash* to communicate di-

rectly with administration authorities recently resulted in a move
of inter-island political significance. For the last few years there
has been some dissatisfaction among the outer islanders concerning the frequency and quality of administration trading ship service within the Yap District. Several Satawalese on a visit to Truk
asked the administrator of that district, in the name of the *tamol-
nipüsash,* if Lamotrek, Elato, and Satawal could not be incorporated into the Truk District, for, they said, these islands had closer
kin ties to the islands of that district than they did to the islands
of the Yap area. The Truk District administrator forwarded this
request to the Yap District office and the latter inquired about
these feelings in the course of the next field trip. In doing so,
though, the administrator first mentioned the subject to the Ulithian
chief on Mogmog. As a result, the Ulithian *tamol* sent one of the
high-ranking chiefs of the atoll with the administrator to visit
Satawal and Lamotrek. As would be expected, when this chief
made his inquiries of the chiefs of the latter islands, all denied
that they wished to secede from the Yap District. The movement
—which did not have the sanction of the traditional chiefs in the
first place and probably would never have gained it—died with
the inquiries of a high-ranking chief of the traditional inter-island
organization.

One of the most obvious changes which has occurred in Western Carolinian culture since contact with Europeans lies in the
area of religious conversion. As mentioned in Chapter 5, the power
of inter-island *yalus* and magic was often used as a justification and
sanction for enforcing traditional inter-island exchange and tribute
practices, not only between Yap and the outer islands, but also
between the outer islands themselves. Nevertheless, as further discussion has shown, most of these exchange patterns have persisted
while the religion has changed. The analysis to follow will also
show that religious conversion on these islands was primarily politically motivated and occurred within the framework of traditional
political manipulation. Thus, the change was more superficial than
fundamental, at least as far as the alteration of rules of behavior
are concerned.

Roman Catholic missionaries began visiting Lamotrek, Elato, and
Satawal with regularity during the Japanese period of administration (Kaneshiro 1950:2). Their visits on most of the outer islands
were limited to the duration of the ship's layover, but occasionally

a priest would remain on one island for several months between visits of the ship. During World War II missionaries were excluded from the area, thus the total number of converts made on Lamotrek, Elato, and Satawal was small. In the years immediately preceding the war the *sawei* exchange partner of Lamotrek, Elato, and Satawal on Yap was converted to Christianity and as a result no longer demanded that exchange with the three outer islands continue. This, as well as the war itself, did much to break down the bonds between Yap and these islands, but it did not sever ties completely, for tribute payments continued to be sent via Ulithi to the chief of Gatchepar when demanded. After the war missionaries re-entered the area, and a Jesuit mission station was established on Ulithi. A similar station was also built on Puluwat, but since this island lies within the Truk District the priest there had little contact with the more western islands. The Ulithian priest, however, began to accompany the trading ship on its quarterly visits to the other outer islands and occasionally he too might lay over on one of the other outer islands for three months between voyages. But the early converts he made on Lamotrek, Elato, and Satawal were neither numerous nor influential. By 1950 there were about 25 Christians on Lamotrek and no more than five each on Elato and Satawal. And nearly all of these converts were either persons from one of the nonchiefly clans or individuals in chiefly clans who had been converted before rising to positions of power.

On Lamotrek, at least, there was never any organized attempt to control or discourage the inroads of conversion. This is understandable in the context of the indigenous religious beliefs, which emphasized two groups of specialists—mediums and craftsmen—who actively participated in religious ceremonies. These were the individuals who interpreted the attitudes of the *yalus* so there was no need for the total community to understand or reach decisions regarding the workings of ghosts and spirits. Catholicism, as introduced in the islands, did not entail a radical change from these traditional practices, with the exception of a degree of individual participation on the part of all converts. On the whole, though, the convert did not have to undergo a complete reorganization of thought or behavior in order to be accepted as a Christian.

In 1953 the process of little to modest conversion on Lamotrek, Satawal, and Elato changed to mass conversion. Within 18 months the total populations of the first two islands and 90 per cent of the people on the latter had become Christian. The move toward mass conversion began on Lamotrek, when the Christians of the island decided, as a group, that some attempt should be made to convert the total population. Undoubtedly, the fact that Christianity was making extensive inroads on Yap and Ulithi played a part in this decision, for, as most outer islanders knew, it would be prudent to keep pace with the developments of these politically superior islands. One of the most important converts on Lamotrek at that time was the *tamolnipiisash*. The Christians decided that the best course of action would be to ask the Christian chiefs (and the priest) on Ulithi to send someone to Lamotrek to teach the new religion, and as things turned out a more effective move probably could not have been made. The Ulithian chiefs readily agreed, and the next ship which arrived at Lamotrek brought two Ulithian instructors, who then informed the chiefs and the population of the island of their mission. The superiority of the Ulithians within the inter-island status hierarchy was such that no one voiced an objection. Thus, after three months of instruction the *tamolùfalu* of Lamotrek called a meeting of the whole population to discuss the new religion and potential conversion. The Ulithians were present at this meeting. The chiefs and representatives of all lineages decided that conversion would be for the best, and as there were no objections from other residents the new religion was adopted. Today Christianity functions smoothly on the island, and in fact one of its prime supporters, as a lay functionary, is the man who was once the senior male medium.

The political implications of this religious conversion are apparent. Although one cannot claim that the Ulithians, by virtue of their political supremacy within the Yapese political network, forced the outer islanders to convert—and in fact it is doubtful that they were seriously concerned about the outer islanders' religious feelings until the above mentioned request was made— still there is little doubt that wholesale conversion on this island would never have occurred if the suggestions had come from anyone other than a Ulithian or someone in a similarly high status. Evidence which was gathered on Satawal and Elato supports this conclusion. The paramount chief of Satawal first heard of the mass conversion on Lamotrek when the Ulithian instructors stopped at his island on their way home. When I interviewed this chief he told me that he then decided that the people of Satawal should convert in order to be in harmony with those of Lamotrek. Therefore, he asked the Ulithians to return to Satawal and instruct its residents, which they did three months later. On Satawal, as on Lamotrek, a meeting was held at the end of the instructional period and everyone decided to change to Christianity. I asked the chief about the attitudes of the mediums at that time and he said that one of the three then active on the island did not wish to change, but, he said, "I told her that she must and she did."

At this time on Elato few people had yet converted. Unlike the situation on Lamotrek and Satawal, no Ulithians ever came to Elato as religious instructors. Several Lamotrekans subsequent to their own conversion did, however. And as Lamotrek is the superior island of the immediate area—as was shown in the organization of the *Hü*—within a few months 90 per cent of the population had also changed. Even though the paramount chief of Lamotrek is also the chief of Elato, there is no evidence that she ever attempted to influence the Elatoans directly in their decision. The 10 per cent on Elato who did not change—and at the time of my field work were still non-Christian—are an interesting group. One was a very old woman whose age alone gave her enough prestige to withstand the pressures of the lay missionaries from Lamotrek. The others included two men who originally came from Woleai, and their wives and children. Woleai is an island equal, if not superior, to Lamotrek in status. When I asked one of these men why he had not become a Christian as had the rest of the islanders, he replied that on Woleai his kin group was still not Christian, so he saw no reason to change.

The history of conversion on these three islands supports several conclusions already suggested in previous chapters of this work. Religion cannot be considered a fundamental dimension of the network of inter-island ties, although religious beliefs certainly tend to support and agree with the inter-island organization. Conversion has shown, though, that the ties persist even when the new dogma gives no support to the inter-island hierarchical organization. If religion had been the binding force there is every reason to expect disintegration of the system as soon as the supernatural sanctions were removed. But, as is apparent in the act of conversion itself, inter-island ties are still politically strong. When change was suggested by a Ulithian there was no hesitancy on the part of the outer islanders to follow his suggestion, which carried the weight of an order. Since the channels of traditional political organization are still active and important, the attempt at conversion succeeded as soon as the effort was directed into them. The true binding forces of inter-island organization, including the sanctions, would seem to lie outside the field of religion. As I have attempted to demonstrate, they are most important in the area of economic interdependence, which is not only necessary for an even distribution of goods, but also for survival itself in an environment which is often unpredictable.

SUMMARY

The system of socioeconomic ties which exists between Lamotrek, Elato, and Satawal is based on exchange of goods, rights, and personnel. If Lamotrek, as the island of superior status, is taken as the point of focus, the exchange can be diagrammed as follows:

From Lamotrek	To Lamotrek
Gifts (tobacco, trade goods)	Gifts (steel, *rang*, etc.)
Tur, holühol, tobacco (money, foreign goods)	Canoes
Personnel (spouses, children)	Personnel (spouses, children)
Exploitation rights	Tribute
Food (in emergencies)	Food (in emergencies)

Since reciprocity—whether between individuals, kin groups, or islands—must be maintained, the system is self-perpetuating, especially in the area of exchange of rights and personnel, for the balancing of exchange may be delayed for a number of years or even a generation.

It is not entirely clear if the triadic dualism apparent in island-level organization permeates the organization on an inter-island level, but it would seem so. When a Lamotrekan, for example, is asked to describe the inter-island system he will usually speak of his own island in terms of those islands (Ulithi, Yap) of higher status and those (Satawal, Elato) of lower standing. Lessa (1950: esp. 31, 39) notes the same orientation on the part of the Ulithian when he speaks of Yap on the one hand and Woleai on the other —with Ulithi in between.

In any case the inter-island system, as island-level organization, is flexible enough to adapt readily to changing circumstances without altering fundamental social organization. The ease with which the outer islands adjusted to foreign rule with a minimum of internal conflict would certainly seem to support this conclusion.

8

Summary and Conclusions

In this work I have attempted to delineate a complex of socio-economic ties which unite the populations of Lamotrek, Elato, and Satawal into a single social system. The evidence which has been presented would seem to indicate that these same ties were the basis of the Yapese political network, which functioned in the Western Carolines in pre-contact times. For in both cases the systems were dependent on a framework of economic and symbolic exchange between a hierarchy of ranked lineages, subclans, clans, and islands. Certain environmental characteristics of the area have probably encouraged the system of economic exchange to develop and endure in order that the populations of individual islands could be assured of survival in times of crisis. Foremost of the environmental conditions are the prevalence of tropical storms and typhoons, the susceptibility of low coral islands to damage by such storms, and the infertile coraline soils, which support a meager resource base.

The coral islands of the Western Carolines which I have discussed are inhabited by small populations divided into numerous discrete social groups—descent lines, lineages, subclans, and clans. Natural or unusual phenomena could easily eliminate some of these groups from the social system. For example, a predominance of male births in one generation, or the accidental loss of a canoe at sea might lead to the extinction of a particular lineage or even clan on a given island. Satawal—the island with the largest popula-

170

tion of the three discussed—has around 300 inhabitants, while Elato is populated by less than 50 individuals. The populations of these islands are divided among eight and five clans, respectively, and these are further subdivided into subclans and lineages. If the inhabitants of these two islands were equally divided among all clans —which by no means is the case—the clans on Satawal would average 40 individuals and those on Elato 10. The eight clans of Lamotrek, if equally represented, would have some 25 members each. Even if these units were not further subdivided, as they are, it is easy to see how quickly one of these groups might be decimated. Thus, in addition to the pattern of economic exchange which has developed between these islands, a system of personnel exchange (marriage and adoption) and alternative acceptable methods of inheritance and tenure have arisen.

There is evidence to suggest that in the past the populations of these islands were considerably larger. Undoubtedly, though, the groups which originally settled these islands were smaller than those which now inhabit them. And even in the period of maximum population the number of inhabitants could not have been so large as to be completely immune to the conditions stated above. If one did not have recourse to genealogical information it would be easy to assume that the various rules governing inheritance and tenure (i.e., matrilineal, patrilateral, adoptive, and gift) are the result of recent developments, specifically depopulation brought about by contact with foreign powers. For, indeed, the existence of alternative rules often leads to disputes which one would expect to be symptomatic of a general breakdown in traditional organization. But, more important, the existence of alternative rules permits an orderly transmission of land and rights no matter how great the imbalance of population units may be at any one time as a result of phenomenal alterations during the preceding generations. Human survival on small islands often depends on a maximum exploitation of available resources. Emergencies, as those that have been mentioned above, may take large areas of the island out of production for extended periods of time. Other areas of the island, where cultivation may not have been justified previously and whose production might have been considered surplus, can rapidly become production which spells the difference between survival and starvation. A situation such as this encourages a system of continual ownership of all land areas, and thus recognition of alternative means for transmitting land from person to person or group to group with a minimum of dispute. And, in addition, lineage, subclan, and clan land holdings become dispersed, not only on individual islands, but also between islands.

Alternative rules of inheritance most often are put into effect during a period of depopulation. Any increase in the number of land disputes which results is not likely to become serious, since at that time there will probably be no great pressure for land. When disputes do arise, though, they are usually settled in formalized ways before they break into open conflict. During a period of population increase the importance of actual residence increases. Residence on a homestead and exploitation of its associated plots may make the difference between ownership recognized as valid by the community and that which is not. If the representatives of a particular subclan on one island are unwilling to extend a claim through residence to the land of that subclan on another island—when the lineage representing it there expires—then this land may pass on patrilaterally, adoptively, or on the basis of gift and residence. It is more important for the total community that the land be cultivated and exploited than for it to remain unexploited and within the more legitimate confines of matrilineality. In most cases, though, subclans will attempt to exercise all potential inheritance rights by residence. Thus, subclans tend to disperse and settle on more than one island.

Intraclan marriage cannot be considered a recent development, either. Genealogical evidence suggests that such marriages were occurring before there was any significant turn toward depopulation which might have been induced by contact with Western powers. Intraclan marriage can be viewed as a developmental process which will eventually result in the emergence of new clans. There is a natural tendency for some social units to grow in number just as others may decrease in size. And when the former become too large—as seems to be the case on Lamotrek, where over 50 per cent of the population belongs to a single clan—fission of that unit is likely to occur, probably along subclan lines. Eventually one could expect the new unit to adopt a new name.

Lessa (1950:50-51 fn.) quotes D. M. Schneider as being impressed with the way in which Yapese culture has adjusted to changing conditions which are the outgrowth of colonial rule. This comment would be equally valid with respect to outer island culture. The adjustment is not so unusual, though, if one recognizes that the potential for adaptation is a basic dimension of their social organization. The demands of foreign powers have been met in the same way that any other alteration of the environment would have been met. It is quite likely that this adaptability is directly related to the triadic/dualistic organization, for, as Lévi-Strauss (1963:151) has commented, this type of organization is universally dynamic.

The disorganization or reorganization one might have expected due to Western intervention are minimal for the above reasons and because of the colonial emphasis which has transcended changes in administrations. First, initial contact with foreigners was infrequent and based on trade—a familiar feature of local organization. Prolonged face-to-face contact has remained infrequent and even today averages only four times a year. Second, those individuals who have traveled beyond the outer islands have not been able to return with material goods which would significantly alter local exploitation patterns. And travel in itself is not impressive, for not only did aboriginal *pelu* have the ability to do the same but aboriginal organization necessitated voyages to Yap and Guam, where contact was made with cultures substantially different from that of the outer islands. Copra is the primary outer island resource which has value in a world market. Coconut trees were a crop already intensively cultivated on all islands and a crop which produced a surplus on most. Exploitation of this crop for commercial purposes did not entail any fundamental organizational changes in ownership or methods of cultivation, but only a change in labor emphasis. The absorption of money into local economic organization was little more than the transferral of value from other mediums of exchange familiar to the outer islanders.

Political change thus far brought about by foreign intervention has not been extensive for similar reasons. The level of sociocultural integration reached in the Western Carolines was of a supra-island level, a level where islands of different rank and of a qualitatively different organization—as in the case of Yap—were tied together via recognized channels of exchange and communication. This permitted, as far as the outer islands were concerned, a smooth transition and integration of foreign powers into the system. As long as the colonial power could be dealt with through channels already established in outer island social organization there would be no reason to expect their influence to result in far-reaching cultural changes in these societies. The colonial powers, for all practical purposes, have been substituted for the authority of Yap, especially on the level of economic exchange. These foreign powers, though, have not been able to provide any greater insurance of survival on an island level than did Yap; thus, there is no reason to abandon the ties which exist between smaller and closer groupings of islands since they remain an essential element of survival.

Under these circumstances the greatest potential for change comes from two sources. On the one hand it comes from Ulithi, which can exert its influence along traditional lines and which is able to increase its power with respect to the other outer islands by virtue of its more frequent and direct contact with the administering government. As long as Ulithi feels safe from any reprisals Yap might make, this island can continue to influence the outer islands to its own advantage—if it so desires. Traditional channels of communication meant that the other outer islanders always dealt with the highest authority through Ulithi. And since the present administration usually relays policy decisions or institutes pilot projects on that island before attempting similar measures on the other outer islands, this pattern is still followed. The second source for potential cultural change comes from the *tamolnïpüsash,* whose power may increase as his face-to-face contact with administrators does. Thus far, though, the most apparent change in Western Carolinian organization has been in the area of religion, and even this was brought about through traditional political manipulation. Christianity as adopted and practiced on the outer islands cannot be considered a really fundamental alteration of traditional organization. Changes in the realms of economic, kinship, and political organization have been held to a minimum because, thus far, outside influence in these areas has been channeled along lines already familiar to the culture and because a supra-island level of sociocultural integration existed aboriginally.

Epilogue, 1989

In the twenty-five years that have passed since the research for this book was completed I have had the opportunity to undertake an additional three and one-half years of fieldwork on several neighboring atolls and islands of Micronesia and briefly revisit Lamotrek in 1965, 1976, 1980, and 1987. It will not surprise anyone that numerous particulars of life on Lamotrek and throughout the region have changed. Many of the older residents who played key roles in the preceding discussion have since died, including chiefs Tagilimal (plate 8), Ligiol (plate 9), and Igefail (plate 10), while others mentioned, including Mahoa (Magowe) and Reieg (plate 40), have succeeded them. Happily, Lefaioup (plate 7) continues as paramount chief, alternating her residence, as in earlier years, between Lamotrek and Elato.

Many of the routines of daily life have not significantly changed. In this respect, the substance of the comments that opened this book (pages 2-4) are still applicable. Specifically, the types and pace of social and cultural change on Lamotrek reflect the realities of survival on a coral atoll — these are realities that severely limit adaptive choices. Nevertheless, some important organizational and behavioral changes have occurred or are in process on the island. Foremost among these are changes that derive from the increasing importance of money within the economy and alterations in the political structure of the state of Yap and Micronesia.

EXTERNAL INFLUENCES: MONEY AND GOVERNMENT

The annual budget appropriated by the United States Congress for the administration of the Trust Territory began to rapidly escalate in the

Plate 44 A group of men seated near the new dispensary on Lamotrek, 1987. Foreground (l. to r.): Magowe (listed as Mahoa in plate 40; he also appears in the frontispiece), Taro (with glasses, also is seen in plate 38), and Tilimai (with back to camera). Background: Rangmal and Wilitifil (with beard).

mid-1960s. The seven and one-half million dollars deemed sufficient in 1961 grew to thirty-five million in 1968 and nearly 100 million by 1987. These new monies, for the most part, have been spent on the main islands of each district (now state), expanding and improving the infra-structure of government buildings, housing, hospitals, roads, airports, docks, sewers, and power plants. Some of the money has "trickled down" to the outer islands and in those more remote areas, where the 1960s per capita annual income was less than twenty dollars, even a meager trickle has resulted in a significant proportional increase.

Most of that money has arrived as wages and salaries for government employees. In the early 1960s, for example, local teachers and health workers received no salaries. They were solely recompensed by their own communities. In most cases (Lamotrek among them), the compensation was in the form of periodic contributions of food, donated in rotation by the households of the island, and exemption from other communal labor duties. By the late 1960s, however, these individuals were receiving salaries from the Yap District Education or Health Departments. One or two such salaries easily exceeded the total income (derived almost entirely from copra sales) of all other residents put together.

Government money was also spent in the outer islands on new school buildings and additional staff. The timber and thatch elementary school of Lamotrek (plate 34) was replaced in the early 1970s by a concrete block structure and enlarged to eight grades that were staffed by four full-time teachers. The dispensary and church were similarly rebuilt although these projects were financed by non-government (although largely external) funds.

Plate 45 The new concrete and metal roofed school, 1976.

The market for wage labor on Yap proper also grew as money became more plentiful. Although outer islanders found they were still discriminated against on that island, many men did find opportunities there for short-term unskilled work, most commonly as stevedores or day-laborers. Such men circulated between their home communities and Madrid, the ghetto-like outer islander settlement on the fringes of Colonia. Others gained more long-term employment on one of the two ships that serve the district — the M/V Micro Spirit (the field trip successor to the M/V Errol) or the M/V Caroline Islands (a supply ship servicing Yap, Pohnpei and other districts). By the 1980s, in fact, nearly all berths on these ships, from field trip, deck and engineering officers to engine wiper and mess-boy had been filled by outer islanders, several of whom were from Lamotrek.

Policy changes during these years not only saw most of the Americans of the Trust Territory administration replaced by Micronesians, but also each of the Trust Territory's remaining four districts (Yap, Truk, Pohnpei, and Kosrae) became internally self-governing states within the newly constituted Federated States of Micronesia (FSM). Each state developed its own constitution, which, in the Yap case, provided outer islanders with several political channels for direct access to, and some guaranteed employment in, the state government.

Yap was divided into ten electoral districts, four of which are in the outer islands. One of these is made up of Lamotrek-Elato-Satawal, the three islands traditionally labeled Lamotrekalaplap, 'Greater Lamotrek'; the participants of the *Hü*. The administrative branch of the state government (patterned after American models) is headed by a governor and lieutenant governor. The state constitution stipulates that when one of these offices is filled by a Yapese, the other must be held by an outer islander. Although theoretically it is possible for an outer islander to be elected governor it is unrealistic to expect this given the population distribution within the state. Therefore, the office of lieutenant governor, first held by a Ulithian and now by a Woleaian, is the highest office guaranteed an outer islander. Several of the administrative divisions of the government are similarly demarcated. The education department, for example, has separate branches dealing with the two geographic subdivisions of the state.

In addition, an administrative subdistrict center was established on Falalop, Ulithi, where a Ulithian Governor's Representative (GOVREP) heads several outer islands branch offices of state government departments and agencies. The most important of these is the Outer Islands High School (OIHS). Most communications between Yap and the farther outer islands consequently are routed through the office of the Ulithi GOVREP. One might recall that at the end of Chapter 8, I speculated that externally induced change on Lamotrek most likely would flow through Ulithi, where its residents were ideally positioned to act as brokers to the outside world.

The modern state government is articulated with the traditional in several ways. The chiefs of both Yap and the outer islands hold membership, respectively, on either the Council of Pilung (Yap) or the Council of Tamol (Outer Islands). These bodies can advise the elected officials and veto any legislation they believe infringes on their customary powers. Members of these councils also have a strong voice in selecting or approving candidates who run for the elective offices. The chairman or head of the Council of Tamol is a Ulithian chief who resides at Madrid on Yap. In this respect, once again, Ulithi has maintained its important intermediary position between Yap and the other outer islands.

ECONOMIC, SOCIAL AND POLITICAL CHANGE ON LAMOTREK

Subsistence Changes

On Lamotrek the new money and governmental structure have affected a number of traditional subsistence activities. For example, the large number of youths away at school or work has reduced those locally available for community labor. This has resulted in a shift from cooperative activities, such as surround-net (*yating*) fishing, toward greater reliance on individual techniques, like hook-and-line or trap fishing.

Further, the influx of money has permitted those residents with adequate income to buy outboard motors and boats. Initially these boats were purchased from builders on Yap or Ulithi. By the mid-1970s, however, some Lamotrek men had learned the necessary construction techniques and were producing them locally. Now even these craft are being phased out in favor of fiberglass models — once again built on Yap. A serious consequence of this trend, of course, is that the younger men of Lamotrek now have fewer opportunities to learn the techniques of traditional canoe construction and carpentry.

The use of boats and motors has tended to shift fishing away from the reef and lagoon to the open ocean and to the nearby uninhabited islands of Lamaliur and Olimarao. Open ocean trolling for tuna occurs much more commonly than in the 1960s, when fishermen were wholly dependent on favorable winds. Turtle hunters, too, now find it easier and less risky to travel to Olimarao and Lamaliur. The boats they use are usually

Plate 46 Construction underway on a boat near Urieitakh canoe house, 1976.

equipped with a walky-talky or C.B. radio that permits them to keep in touch with each other as well as the residents of Lamotrek. In this way emergencies can be dealt with much more quickly than in the past. These production gains should be judged in the light of possible iosses.

Although no quantitative data were collected, in 1976 my observations suggested that the use of motor boats had resulted in a significant increase in the number of turtles harvested from Lamaliur and Olimarao. In time this could seriously deplete the long-range stock of turtles. Furthermore, as fishermen and hunters turn to mechanized craft (and the larger canoes disappear), they become more dependent on the uninterrupted supply of gasoline and motors for their survival.

These changes in fishing patterns have resulted in differential access to marine resources by some members of the community. The former communal and cooperative expeditions guaranteed that all households obtained fish at least once a week. Now, those households with no youths in residence, or where there is no wage earner, often have limited access to boats and motors. These residents receive fish less regularly than in former years. Such households have to depend on the labor of less active older men, who in turn are forced to rely on fish traps and angling for their catches.

The subsistence contributions of women have been less affected by these "modernization" trends. Taro and breadfruit remain the vegetable staples of the Lamotrek diet, but the percentage of purchased foods consumed has increased as the amount of locally available money has grown. Rice, canned meat, and canned fish are eaten more frequently and in larger quantities than in the 1960s. Lamotrek residents now say they are attracted to these foods not only because they are desirable "luxuries," but also because they are "convenient." The range of purchased products has also grown. Flour, yeast, refined sugar, coffee, soft-drink powders, and even sacked onions and the current "food fad" of frozen turkey tails, are regularly purchased. Several of these products have contributed to a deterioration in the nutritional character of the diet especially among children where caries, once rare, are now a serious problem.

Sociopolitical Change

Money has begun to complicate the exercise of chiefly authority. Chiefly power derives from the control of land and territory. Money is a resource not often controlled by chiefs or their lineages since it originates off-island. Chiefly authority is primarily validated by genealogy. As money competes with land as an important source of power, achieved status (derived from externally acquired knowledge) will likely weaken the genealogically ascribed positions of the traditional polity. Of course ability and knowledge were also traditionally important sources of power (as in the cases of *pelu* or *sennap*), but not in defining chiefly authority. Nevertheless, it is interesting to note, that at least one individual on Lamotrek who is in line to succeed to a chiefly position, has taken special care to go on to high school even though he was in his mid-thirties when he began his studies. In so doing, he believes he has augmented his status on the island and strengthened his claim to such an office when it comes available. Selection of the 'chief for the foreigners' (*tamolyapisash*) from among the island's four chiefs may eventually depend on acquiring these modern skills — although it might also be argued that the need for such a chief has decreased since "foreigners" in the government have been replaced by Yapese and other Micronesians.

Even those with modest schooling and money derive a degree of prestige from the trappings and material patina of the outside world. Students, workers, and visitors to Yap return with material evidence of their travels ranging from tee shirts and watches, to tape recorders, pellet guns, and even motor bikes. The fads, tastes, and styles of the port-towns and cities they have visited also return with them. Young men, for example, vaunt new styles of dress and decoration, even in loincloths. Those who have attended school on Ulithi return wearing loincloths twice as long as those normally worn by men on Lamotrek. These modish *tur* are wound and draped in a manner that covers the buttocks and thighs (plate 47). Older

Plate 47 Changing dress styles among the men, 1976. Youths who have attended high school on Ulithi return wearing long, draping loin cloths.

residents — some amused and some offended by this affectation — tease or criticize those who continue to dress in this way.

Among adult men, money has changed the type and quantity of alcoholic beverages consumed and to some extent, this has resulted in some recent challenges to chiefly authority. Most of the yeast purchased is not used in baking, but in brewing. A beer concocted from a mixture of yeast, sugar, and rice-water now supplements or has replaced palm wine among some drinkers. Recipes and techniques of brewing are two of the extra-curricular talents picked up by youths who have been away to school on Ulithi, Guam, and Pohnpei. There they have also developed a taste for commercial beer and liquor, which is frequently bootlegged to the outer islands via the field trip ship.

The chiefs of Lamotrek continue to prohibit the importation of alcohol but, since the ship is manned by friends and relatives, it is very difficult to control the private cargoes of "deck or engine room entrepreneurs." Although the trading companies are not licensed to sell alcohol in the outer islands, cases of beer have been found in the ship's hold mistakenly labeled "soft drinks." At Lamotrek through the 1970s and into the 1980s beer and liquor were not openly off-loaded, as the chiefs were quite strict in enforcing this prohibition. Some of the island's young men, however, have taken advantage of a perceived "loophole" in the edict. They obtain beer and liquor aboard ship and drink it before returning to shore, while bobbing about the lagoon in a small flotilla of boats and canoes. The chiefs were not amused by this exceedingly legalistic interpretation of their prohibition and they may have since clarified their intentions.

Social Change: Males and Females

Most of the externally induced changes that have altered life on Lamotrek have been introduced by and directly linked to the men of the island. Few women have gone away to school or work. Formal schooling for women is still largely limited to that available on the island itself. Members of the community most commonly explain that girls are not sent away because residents fear they will return pregnant. The lower status of Lamotrek in comparison to Ulithi, where the Outer Islands High School is located, suggests to them that it would be difficult for most Lamotrek girls to resist any advances made by higher ranking Ulithian men. The small number of Lamotrek girls who have attended that school are ones with close relatives on Ulithi with whom they could live or girls who have been accompanied by chaperons who take up residence near the school in a Woleai-Lamotrek residential compound.

The lineage structure of the society appears to be another compelling reason women less frequently leave the island than men. Lineage solidarity on Lamotrek is based on the complementary roles and contributions of males and females. The core units of the lineage are its cross-sibling (brother-sister) sets. Within those units, the women (sisters) are the main links to the land. Women not only are the main agricultural workers, but it is through them — in this matrilineal and matrilocal society — that land is accessed and transmitted. Men leave their lineage lands when they marry; they retain access to that land by defending and "speaking for" their sisters. There exists, then, an implied or "understood" social contract between brothers and sisters: women who anchor the lineage to the land and men who are publicly responsible for guarding and protecting such rights. Under these circumstances, women are discouraged from leaving the island because their absence threatens the unity of the set and its ties to the land, which might lapse if they did not return.

The system is already strained because so many men are absent and unable to fulfill their guardianship duties. Some Lamotrek residents, consequently, have concluded that off-island education and employment are mixed blessings. Although new knowledge and money can benefit the lineage, the loss of key personnel can also place kin groups at a disadvantage, especially if those missing members marry while away and never return. Many who do return from such places as Guam, Honolulu or Los Angeles, often find it difficult to readapt to the "quiet" life of the outer islands. These youths, who frequently have lost their traditional skills and physical endurance, find they have become marginal participants in local subsistence pursuits and decision making when their expectations were that their experiences and training would increase their power. From the point of view of the permanent residents, however, their training has little relevance to the daily problems of survival on the atoll. Many such youths feel isolated and have become increasingly discouraged, embittered, or alcoholic.

Socioeconomic Change: Entrepreneurs

A more immediate, threat to the traditional order of Lamotrek probably can be traced to an emerging "class" of entrepreneurial storekeepers. In the 1960s the only store on the island was the communally owned cooperative. Cooperative stores were promoted by the government to expedite trade during the visit of the field trip ship. A single bulk-buyer at each island could be dealt with more efficiently than a multitude of small purchasers who otherwise descended upon the ship at each stop. The residents of each island were told to pool their money and found a co-op, which obtained goods on the ship at wholesale prices. Those purchases were resold on the island at retail prices and the profit realized was reinvested in the co-op or in some other community oriented project.

Beginning in the late 1960s, however, the newly salaried teachers, health aides, and ship's officers have often used their incomes to open competing retail stores. Outer islanders who have visited Yap or other port-towns are convinced that storekeepers gain wealth and power without much work — certainly with less than that required in traditional subsistence pursuits. For these individuals owning a store is seen as a way to become rich and powerful as well as gain immediate and consistent access to cheaper imported goods. As a consequence the co-op has gone bankrupt. The capital for the co-op was raised from the community as a whole. Therefore that store had to treat all residents equally. When credit was extended to one resident, it had to be available to all. When the inventory of the co-op was depleted, residents had to turn to the private stores for imported items. Those private stores only extended credit to the close kin of the store owner. In this way the cash circulating within the community gradually flowed into the private stores while the debts owed the co-op remained unpaid. Soon the co-op no longer had sufficient capital to renew its inventory. The private stores, having extended less credit, could survive longer on uncollected debts because their salaried owners infused new capital from government paychecks to renew inventories.

Intra-community discord is one noticeable consequence of this situation. Some residents find themselves increasingly indebted and "hostage" to the private stores. Storekeepers are privately (and occasionally openly) accused of stinginess and greed. Many residents try to limit their trade to related storekeepers or to those who live in the same district. The difficulties persist, however, and cross-currents of tension within and between kin groups and districts are growing. In 1976, for example, I found that discord between the north and south had reached such a level that a number of residents in these respective districts were reluctant to visit friends in the other except under the most pressing of circumstances. They were fearful that visits would provoke "trouble" on the island. This calls to mind the social rivalries of the past that resulted in similar district isolation and which were said to have encouraged the development of the north-south dialect differences.

Inter-Island Political Change

Challenges to the traditional inter-island political order are also in progress. Lamotrek's claims of control over the resources on Olimarao, Pikh, and Pikhailo have been openly questioned by Elato and Satawal in recent years, just as Ulithi's claim to a degree of authority over "the Woleai" and Lamotrekalaplap has been challenged by residents of the latter two regions.

This trend can be seen most clearly within the newly constituted and popularly elected government. In traditional times, Ulithi's influence over the more distant outer islands derived in part from its proximity to Yap. The chiefs of Ulithi, could control most communication between Yap and the other outer islands. As already mentioned, if Ulithi continues to evolve as a sub-district (or state) center, it will secure a similar key position in the new governmental structure. However, perhaps in recognition of this, some of the more distant outer islands have tried to alter this power differential by nominating their own candidates to offices in the state and FSM governments. Since the number of voters in the Woleai and Lamotrekalaplap outnumber those of Ulithi-Fais, Ulithians have been replaced in the last two elections by Woleaians, both as Lt. Governor on Yap and as the outer island senator in the Congress of Micronesia (this senator, in fact, has now risen to become President of the Federated States of Micronesia).

The power of Lamotrek within Lamotrekalaplap has similarly been challenged by Satawal. This precinct was first represented by a Lamotrek man in the Yap State legislature, but recently Satawal has used its larger population to elect its own candidate. Many people on Lamotrek, of course, feel threatened by this development.

Perhaps it is inevitable that one reaction to such changes has been an attempt to "revive the past," emanating in large part, from the traditionally chartered centers of power. Within the Yap State legislature outer islands representatives find they are under some pressure to agree to *ad hoc* alliances with the Gagil delegate who represents their former *sawei* "overlords." Some of the Gagil *sawei*, in fact, have expressed an interest in revitalizing communication with the outer islanders. In 1980, Lamotrek and Ifaluk's *sawei* visited her outer island "children" for the first time in more than twenty years (plate 48). Similarly, various chiefs of Ulithi, Woleai and Lamotrek have become more vocal in defending their authority and in attempting to enforce tradition. The Council of Tamol is the principal forum for these interests, but on Lamotrek itself I noted

Plate 48 Moroy, Lamotrek's Yapese *sawei*, visits Lamotrek in 1980.

a number of rituals and ceremonial activities that appeared threatened in the 1960s had re-emerged in the 1970s and 1980s. In 1980, for example, the funeral restrictions on consumption and exploitation were more diligently enforced than those observed in 1962-63 — the sound of the conch shell once again carried across the island at sunrise and sunset signalling the imposition or rescinding of such taboos.

While chiefs are seeking to guard or guarantee their positions some traditional artisans (*maletabw*) are also actively promoting their skills among younger members of the community by encouraging them once again to take an interest in traditional navigation, divination, and curing. On Satawal in 1986, one interesting example of this trend was the founding by Piailug (who has gained fame in the outside world for his traditional navigational abilities during voyages of the Hawaiian *Hokule'a* canoe) of the "University of Satawal," where he hoped to attract youths and teach his traditional skills.

SUMMARY

The people of Lamotrek and the other outer islands are faced with a continually changing and challenging natural and social environment. Many of the natural threats of the past — typhoons, droughts, starvation, and disease — are less immediate today owing to the reliability of relief aid and access to hospital and local medical care. But the number of sociopolitical threats to their cultural cohesion and unity have increased. Money, new forms of competition, and emigration are foremost among them. Of these destabilizing influences the most noticeable effect to date, has been the diminution of the cooperative spirit that once characterized so many activities on Lamotrek. This has been weakened by the differential wealth that has begun to isolate individuals and fragment residential groups and lineages. The traditional authority and power structure of Lamotrek, which is based primarily on control of land and genealogical standing, cannot help but be altered as money and external goods become new sources for power. Efforts are being made by the residents, individually and collectively, to come to grips with these problems. The history of the atoll has demonstrated that its people have successfully adapted to many significant changes in the past and barring any catastrophic events they can probably continue to do so into the future.

ADDITIONAL BIBLIOGRAPHY

I have published a number of additional items on Lamotrek and its neighboring atolls. The following list includes those that deal with topics that were first raised in this book.

1 "Systems of Measurement on Woleai Atoll, Caroline Islands," *Anthropos*, 65:1-73. St. Augustin, Germany. 1970.
2 "Land Tenure in the Woleai," Chapter 3 in *Land Tenure in Oceania*, edited by Henry Lundsgaarde. Honolulu: University of Hawaii Press. 1974.
3 *An Introduction to the Peoples and Cultures of Micronesia*. 2nd edition. Menlo Park, CA: Cummings Publishing Co. 1977.
4 *Coral Islanders*. Arlington Heights, IL: Harlan Davidson Publishing. 1978.
5 "Traditional Exchange Systems and Modern Political Developments in the Yap District of Micronesia," chapter in *Persistence and Exchange*, edited by Roland Force and Brenda Bishop. Honolulu: Pacific Science Assoc. 1981.
6 "The Traditional Classification and Treatment of Illness on Woleai and Lamotrek in the Caroline Islands, Micronesia," *Culture* 2:29-41. Montreal. 1982.

[7] "Archaeological Test Excavations on Faraulep, Woleai and Lamotrek in the Caroline Islands of Micronesia," Report No. 2 in *Pacific Anthropological Records*, No. 35, edited by Y. Sinoto. Co-authored with Keiko Fujimura. Honolulu: Bishop Museum. 1984.

[8] "Central Carolinian Oral Narratives: Indigenous Migration Theories and Principles of Order and Rank," *Pacific Studies*, 7:1-14. Laie, Hawaii. 1984.

Appendix

ORTHOGRAPHY

The use of native terms in this work is kept to a minimum. They are included either for comparative purposes or as an aid in better understanding the system under discussion.

Very little has been published on Western Carolinian atoll linguistics, hence there is no widely accepted orthography. Those publications on the topic which have appeared (see bibliography) are not satisfactory for recording the Lamotrekan dialect. The following symbols are used to record the phonemes indicated.

a	as in f*a*ther	o	as in v*o*te
ä	as in f*a*t	u	as in t*oo*
e	as in f*e*d	ü	as in f*eu* (Fr.)
ë	/e/ with rounded lips	u̇	as in f*u*n
i	as in f*ee*t	l	initially as English,
			medially and terminally
ï	as in f*i*t		close to /d/.
ȯ	as in f*ou*ght	r	is flapped

The sounds /sh/ and /ch/ are allophones of a single phoneme. I have made the distinction in recording them not because of a fundamental difference, but only as an aid to pronunciation. The same is true for the recording of allophones /h/, /g/, and /kh/.

The Lamotrekese word *li*, which can be translated as "of" or "of the," is often contracted to *ü* in compound words. Occasionally it will appear as *nï,* since *n* and *l,* although separate phonemes, are often interchangeable. In all cases I have recorded this particle as it sounds.

Terminal consonants, and especially vowels, are often so lightly voiced in Lamotrekese as to be nearly inaudible; thus in some cases I may not have recognized the presence of such phonemes and failed to record them.

Glossary of Native Terms

This glossary contains all of the Lamotrek vernacular words used in this book. In 1962-63, when the research was carried out, there was no established orthography or standardized spellings for the Lamotrek language. Since that time a dictionary of the closely related Woleai language has appeared (Ho-min Sohn and Anthony F. Tawerilmang, *Woleaian-English Dictionary*, PALI Language Texts, Honolulu: The University Press of Hawaii, 1976). Consequently, wherever possible I have included Woleai renderings of these words in brackets.

aramat [yaramat]. Person.
bulòkh [bulag, bwulog]. Cyrtosperma, an important subsistence root crop. A variety of taro.
bwei [be]. A system of divination whereby omens are derived from numbers of knots tied in strips of coconut frond pinnae.
bwïsi [bisi]. 'My sibling of the same sex.' A kinship term with first person singular suffix.
bwïsùbwïs [bisibis]. 'Sibling of a sibling,' someone who is related "like a sibling of the same sex," (real or classificatory).
bwitokh [bitog]. 'Come here,' in the south dialect of Lamotrek.
bwogat [bwogot, bugot]. A homestead or estate; the people of that land, a lineage, relatives.
bwùl [bol]. An area of taro cultivation, the swampy interior of the island.
bwutokh [buutog]. 'Come here,' in the standard or northern dialect of Lamotrek.
chalugùtug [shoalugutug]. A high ranking position, second to that of a chief, on the island of Elato. Similar in rank and function to ochang.

chùitibwul. A gift offered by biological parents to a couple that adopts one of their children.

erao [yeraw]. Homestead (or estate residence) of a chiefly lineage.

etabw [getabu]. Taboo.

fal-lap [fannap, fenap]. 'Big house.' An island's men's house.

fatui [fatiuw]. Sister's child. A kinship term reciprocal to malalap.

fille [file]. Alocasia or ''elephant ear taro,'' a type of root crop of secondary subsistence importance.

fitiei [fitiya]. My spouse; a kinship term with first person singular suffix.

foto. A type of celebratory dance performed by the men on a canoe returning from a successful reef or lagoon fishing expedition.

hafang [gefang]. A gift.

hailang [gailang]. Matri-clan.

hailul. A type of celebratory dance performed by the men on a canoe returning from a successful open ocean fishing expedition.

harangap [garengaap]. Bonito, a species of pelagic fish.

hatu [gaatu]. Cat.

holimel. A specific section of the Lamotrek reef.

holòkh [gelaag]. Dog.

holùhol [galogal, golugol]. Coconut sennit cordage (of common small to moderate diameter) used for fishing line, lashings, sewing.

hos [gos]. A carved wooden effigy used by navigators. The hos is usually Janus-headed, the two faces representing Pelualap and Yalulawei, the patron spirits of navigation. It takes its name from the four to six sting-ray spines that are fixed to its lower end.

hù [geo] 'Fishhook'. An exchange system that links Lamotrek, Elato, and Satawal.

hùfäs [geffas]. To joke or to clown. An occasion when people entertain the community with joking and clowning behavior.

hurùhur [gurugur]. A wooden staff, named after the orangewood from which it is commonly made, used in the stick dances of men, which probably emulate once practiced fencing techniques of hand-to-hand combat. Such a staff is also an important part of a household altar dedicated to ancestral ghosts.

lai [laiu]. Child; a kinship term.

lailùbwïsi [laiubisi]. 'Child of my sibling of the same sex.' Nephew or niece. A kinship term with first person singular suffix.

Lamotrekalaplap [Lamwocheg Lapelap]. 'Greater Lamotrek,' i.e. Lamotrek, Elato, and Satawal.

lù [liu]. Coconut palms or unripe coconuts used primarily as a source of drinking water.

lukh [lug]. The middle or midpoint. An important conceptual location in a variety of domains.

mai. Breadfruit or breadfruit tree.

malùbwogat [mwalibugot]. 'Man of the homestead (lineage).' The senior male of a lineage or of an estate.

malalap [mwalelap]. 'Big man.' One's mother's brother. A kinship term reciprocal to fatui.

maletabw 'Taboo man.' A qualified specialist in a traditional domain of magico-religious importance.

mälukh [maliug]. Chicken.

malùmei. A first fruits ceremony marking the beginning of the annual breadfruit harvest.

mar. Preserved breadfruit.

mashang. A coconut palm frond taboo sign attached to an object that is subject to confiscation after a taboo has been broken.

mepel [maipil]. 'Religious offering,' a kind of sawei tribute. In the modern context mepel can mean a Christian prayer.

metau [metaw]. The open ocean.

muimuilìmashang. A gift made to a chief in recompense for breaking a taboo.

ngal. Wahoo, a species of pelagic fish.

ngùl [ngel]. Soul.

ochang. A chief's spokesman or helper. A person of relatively high rank, similar to tela.

paliwen [paliuwan]. Price, value; a gift presented at a funeral in recognition of past favors or valuables received from the lineage of the deceased.

paliwenùbwogat. 'Price of the land.' A funeral gift made by a recipient lineage to a donor lineage, when a death occurs in the latter, acknowledging a previously received gift of land.

paliwenùlù. 'Price of the coconut palm.' A funeral gift made by a recipient lineage to a donor lineage, when a death occurs in the latter, acknowledging a previously received gift of a coconut palm.

paliwenùmai. 'Price of the breadfruit.' A funeral gift made by a recipient lineage to a donor lineage, when a death occurs in the latter, acknowledging a previously received gift of a breadfruit tree.

pan-nu [paaniu]. A coconut palm frond.

peigengao. 'Bad [unfortunate] side,' a directional for left.

peigìhatch. 'Good side,' a directional for right.

peigùmal. 'Man's side,' a directional for right.

peigùshabwut. 'Woman's side,' a directional for left.

pelu [paliuw]. A traditionally qualified navigator.

pitigil tamol [pitegaltamol]. 'Things of the chief,' a kind of sawei tribute submitted by the outer islanders to Yap.

rang. Turmeric powder derived from the yellow ginger plant. An important cosmetic applied on most ritual and celebratory occasions.

saoso [sausou]. Sorcery.

sawei [sawey, sawai]. The name for the inter-island socioeconomic exchange system that links the outer islands to Yap. Probably a word of Yapese origin.

sennap [senap]. A traditionally qualified canoe-builder.

shabwuttugofaielibwogat [shabuttugofaiyelibugot]. 'Old woman of the land (lineage).'

shalif. A ritual commemorating a high ranking woman's first pregnancy.

shateng. A funeral ceremony.

sho. Ripe coconuts [copra nuts].

silei [silai]. 'My mother.' A kinship term with first person singular suffix.

silo [siilo]. Pig.

silusilei. 'Mother of my mother,' grandmother. A kinship term with first person singular suffix.

tabw [tapp]. A district of an island.

taho [taguw]. Tuna, a species of pelagic fish.

tamol [tamwel, tamweol]. Chief.

tamollihailang. 'Chief of the clan.' A clan head, usually its senior male.

tamolnipusash [tamweniuyepisash, tamolyapisash]. 'Chief for the foreigner.' An individual designated to act as an island's chief when dealing with foreigners who visit the island. He may or may not be a "true" clan or district chief on his island.

tamolnitabw [tamwenitapp]. 'Chief of the district.' See tabw.

tamolufalu. 'Chief of the island,' a paramount chief.

tamutamai. 'Father of my father,' grandfather. A kinship term with first person singular suffix.

tatibwul. 'Sea-water in the taro swamp.' An occasion when storm waves force saltwater into the taro fields.

tauelipukh. An important channel through the reef of Lamotrek atoll.

tela. 'Adze,' when used metaphorically it refers to a chief's assistant or "voice."

telalihailang. A man who relays or carries instructions from a clan chief or leader to other members of the clan. See tela.

tugakh [tegag]. A belt made of coconut, sea-shell, and turtle shell disks worn by women.

tugutug [tiugiutiug]. A funeral gift.

tumaho [temaag]. Tobacco.

tumailitat [temwaaiutat]. 'Illness of the sea.' An illness emanating from or caused by spirits of the sea.

tur [teor]. A loom-woven banana or hibiscus fiber skirt or loincloth.

ubwut. Immature coconut frond pinnae which are yellow in color. They are essential decorative elements on any ritual occasion.

um [umw]. A ground oven.

uot [wot]. Colocasia, true taro, an important subsistence crop.

waliyalus [waliyalius]. 'Canoe [vehicle] of the spirits.' A medium for spirits or ghosts.

wong. Sea turtle, most commonly the green sea turtle.

yalus [yalius]. Ghost, spirit, or god.

yalusúlang. 'Spirit of the sky.' The most powerful of yalus, a god. Members of this class are frequently patron spirits of important specialized domains.

yalusútat. 'Spirit of the sea.' A powerful class of spirits who frequently cause illness or bring misfortune to an island.

Bibliography

Abbott, R. T.
  1962   *Sea Shells of the World.* Golden Press, New York.
Alkire, W. H.
  1960   "Cultural Adaptation in the Caroline Islands," *Journal of the Polynesian Society,* 69:123-50. Wellington, New Zealand.
Arnow, Ted
  1955   "The Hydrology of Ifaluk Atoll," *Atoll Research Bulletin,* 44: 1-10. Washington, D.C.
Barrau, Jacques
  1958   *Subsistence Agriculture in Melanesia.* Bernice P. Bishop Museum Bulletin 219, Honolulu, Hawaii.
  1951   *Subsistence Agriculture in Polynesia and Micronesia.* Bernice P. Bishop Museum Bulletin 223, Honolulu, Hawaii.
Burrows, Edwin, and M. E. Spiro
  1953   *An Atoll Culture.* Human Relations Area Files, New Haven, Conn.
Damm, H., and E. Sarfert
  1935   *Inseln um Truk.* Ergebnisse der Südsee Expedition 1908-10 (ed. G. Thilenius), II B 6, pt. 2. W. De Gruyter, Hamburg.
Davenport, William
  1964   "Social Structure of the Santa Cruz Islands," *Explorations in Cultural Anthropology* (ed. Ward Goodenough), pp. 57-93. McGraw-Hill, New York.
Elbert, S. H.
  1947a   *Ulithi-English and English-Ulithi Word Lists* (mimeographed). U.S. Naval Military Government, Pearl Harbor, Hawaii.

1947b   *Trukese-English, English-Trukese Dictionary.* U.S. Naval Military Government, Pearl Harbor, Hawaii.

Emerick, R. G.
1958   "Land Tenure in the Marianas," *Land Tenure Patterns Trust Territory of the Pacific Islands,* Vol. 1. Trust Territory Government, Guam.

Emory, K. P.
1944   *South Sea Lore.* Bernice P. Bishop Museum Special Publication 36, Honolulu, Hawaii.

Firth, Raymond
1959   *Economics of the New Zealand Maori.* Government Printer, Wellington, New Zealand.

Fischer, J. L.
1951   *The Eastern Carolines.* Human Relations Area Files, New Haven, Conn.

Fritz, Georg
1911   "Die Zentralkarolinische Sprache," *Lehrbucher des Seminars für Orientalische Sprachen zu Berlin,* Band 29. Berlin.

Geddes, W. R.
1962   "Social Change in Tikopia" (review), *Man,* 62:14-16. London.

Gladwin, Thomas
1962   "Cultural Determinants of Logical Process," *Explorations in Cultural Anthropology* (ed. Ward Goodenough), pp. 167-177. McGraw-Hill, New York.

Gladwin, Thomas, and S. B. Sarason
1953   *Truk: Man in Paradise.* Viking Fund Publication in Anthropology 20, New York.

Goodenough, Ward
1951   *Property, Kin and Community on Truk.* Yale University Press, New Haven, Conn.

1953   *Native Astronomy in the Central Carolines.* University of Pennsylvania Museum, Philadelphia.

1957   "Oceania and the Problem of Controls in the Study of Cultural and Human Evolution," *Journal of the Polynesian Society,* 66:146-55. Wellington, New Zealand.

Haddon, A. C., and James Hornell
1936   *Canoes of Oceania,* 2 vols. Bernice P. Bishop Museum Special Publication 27, Honolulu, Hawaii.

Halstead, B. W.
1959   *Dangerous Marine Animals.* Cornell Maritime Press, Cambridge, Md.

Joseph, Alice, and V. F. Murray
1951   *Chamorros and Carolinians of Saipan.* Harvard University Press, Cambridge, Mass.

Kaneshiro, Shigeru
1950   *Report on Lamotrek* (typescript). Trust Territory Government, Guam.

Krämer, Augustin
    1937   *Zentralkarolinen*. Ergebnisse der Südsee Expedition 1908-10 (ed. G. Thilenius), II B 10, pt. 1. W. De Gruyter, Hamburg.

La Monte, Francesca
    1952   *Marine Game Fishes of the World*. Doubleday and Co., Garden City, New York.

Lessa, W. A.
    1950   "Ulithi and the Outer Native World," *American Anthropologist*, 52:27-52. Menasha, Wisconsin.
    1961a   *Tales from Ulithi Atoll*. Folklore Studies 13, University of California Press, Berkeley.
    1961b   "Sorcery on Ifaluk," *American Anthropologist*, 63:817-20. Menasha, Wisconsin.
    1962a   "The Decreasing Power of Myth on Ulithi," *Journal of American Folklore*, 75:153-59. Lancaster, Pa., and New York City.
    1962b   "An Evaluation of Early Descriptions of Carolinian Culture," *Ethnohistory*, 9:313-403. Bloomington, Ind.

Lessa, W. A., and G. C. Myers
    1962   "Population Dynamics of an Atoll Community," *Population Studies*, 15:244-57. Cambridge.

Lessa, W. A., and M. Spiegelman
    1954   "Ulithian Personality as Seen Through Ethnological Materials and Thematic Test Analysis," *University of California Publication in Culture and Society*, 2:243-301. Berkeley.

Lévi-Strauss, Claude
    1963   *Structural Anthropology*. Basic Books, Inc., New York.

Malinowski, Bronislaw
    1961   *Argonauts of the Western Pacific*. E. P. Dutton, New York.

Mauss, Marcel
    1954   *The Gift* (tr. I. Cunnison). Cohen and West, London.

Murphy, R. E.
    1948   "'High' and 'Low' Islands in the Eastern Carolines," *The Geographical Review*, 37:425-39. New York.

Oliver, Douglas
    1951   *The Pacific Islands*. Harvard University Press, Cambridge, Mass.

Richard, B. E.
    1957   *United States Naval Administration of the Trust Territory of the Pacific Islands*, 2 vols. Office of the Chief of Naval Operations, Washington, D.C.

Riesenberg, Saul, and Shigeru Kaneshiro
    1960   *A Caroline Islands Script*. Bureau of American Ethnology Bulletin 173, Anthropological Papers 60, Washington, D.C.

Schneider, D. M.
    1953   "Yap Kinship Terminology and Kin Groups," *American Anthropologist*, 55:215-36. Menasha, Wisconsin.

Smith, A. G.
    1951   *Gamwoelhaelhi ishilh Weleeya* (Guide to Woleai Spelling) (mimeographed). High Commissioner, Trust Territory of the Pacific Islands, Honolulu, Hawaii.
Spoehr, Alexander
    1954   "Saipan: The Ethnology of a War-Devastated Island," *Fieldiana*, 41. Chicago Natural History Museum.
Steward, Julian H.
    1955   *Theory of Culture Change*. University of Illinois Press, Urbana.
Stillfried, B.
    1953   *Die Soziale Organization in Mikronesien*. Acta Ethnologica et Linguistica 4, Institut für Volkerkunde der Universität Wien.
Stone, B. C.
    1959   "The Flora of Namonuito and the Hall Islands," *Pacific Science*, 13:88-104. Honolulu, Hawaii.
Stone, E. L., Jr.
    1953   "Summary of Information on Atoll Soils," *Atoll Research Bulletin*, 22. Washington, D.C.
Tetens, Alfred
    1958   *Among the Savages of the South Seas: Memoirs of Micronesia, 1862-1868* (tr. F. M. Spoehr). Stanford University Press, Palo Alto, Calif.
Tracey, J. I., D. P. Abbott, and Ted Arnow
    1961   *Natural History of Ifaluk Atoll: Physical Environment*. Bernice P. Bishop Museum Bulletin 222, Honolulu, Hawaii.
Trust Territory of the Pacific Islands
    1960   *Agricultural Report June 4-18. Yap District Outer Islands* (mimeographed). Colonia, Yap.
Uberoi, J. P. Singh
    1962   *Politics of the Kula Ring*. Manchester University Press, Manchester.
Wiens, Herold J.
    1962a   *Atoll Environment and Ecology*. Yale University Press, New Haven, Conn.
    1962b   *Pacific Island Bastions of the United States*. Van Nostrand Co., Princeton, N.J.
Wilson, W., *et al.*
    1799   *A Missionary Voyage to the Southern Pacific Ocean. . . .* T. Chapman, London.
Woodrow, G. Marshall
    1910   *Gardening in the Tropics*. New York.
Zim, Herbert, and H. H. Shoemaker
    1956   *Fishes*. Golden Press, New York.

ISBN 0-88133-399-9

90000